Mary
and the
Eucharist

Fr. Richard Foley, S.J.

 Hope of Saint Monica, Inc.

Cum licentia Superiorum Ordinis

Nihil obstat:	Fr. Anton Cowan Censor
Imprimatur:	Msgr. Tom Egan, V.G. Westminster 8th of September 1997
Nihil obstat:	Reverend Edward J. Gratsch September 28, 1997
Imprimatur:	Most Reverend Carl K. Moeddel Vicar General and Auxiliary Bishop Archdiocese of Cincinnati September 29, 1997

The *Nihil obstat* and *Imprimatur* are a declaration that a book or pamphlet is considered to be free from doctrinal or moral error. It is not implied that those who have granted the *Nihil obstat* or *Imprimatur* agree with the contents, opinions, or statements expressed.

Both the author and the publisher recognize and accept that the final authority regarding reported apparitions or supernatural messages rests with the Holy See, to whose judgment we willingly submit.

Published by: Hope of Saint Monica, Inc.
P.O. Box 308
Newtonsville, Ohio 45158-0308
U.S.A.

Phone: 513-575-5942
Fax: 513-575-5947
Toll-free fax: 888-260-7371

ISBN: 1-891431-00-5
Library of Congress Catalog Card Number: 97-76925

Front cover designed by Mr. Gregory Millar of Manchester, England.

Dedication

This book is dedicated with affection and deep thanks to Sr. Briege McKenna, O.S.C., and Fr. Kevin Scallon, C.M.—two most devoted apostles of the Eucharistic Jesus and Our Lady of the Blessed Sacrament.

Table of Contents

Preface

Mary and the Eucharist—on these mighty twin pillars of Catholic faith and devotion much interest is being focused nowadays. Ours is a Marian age that is fast rediscovering the treasures of the Eucharist.

Hence, indeed, this book. It examines the intimately close working relationship between the Mother of Divine Grace and her Son in the sacrament of the altar. There behind the veils of faith, as during their mortal days, the hearts of Jesus and Mary are united beyond all separation; thus we meet both their loving presences each time we assist at Mass, or receive Holy Communion, or spend time before the tabernacle.

Besides looking at the doctrinal issues involved in this dynamic partnership between Our Lady and the Word-made-Eucharist, my book aims throughout at promoting prayer and kindling devotion. To put this another way, these pages come as much from my heart as from my head; similarly, they are directed both to the minds and hearts of those who read them.

A special word of acknowledgment and thanks is due to my good friend Fr. Michael O'Carroll, C.S.Sp. Besides giving me much personal encouragement, his vast theological learning (especially his encyclopedias on Mary and the Eucharist) has been a wellspring of information and inspiration alike.

Foreword

What an incredible time! As our millennium grinds to a close apparitions of the Blessed Virgin Mary are now joined by an upsurge of devotion to the Blessed Sacrament. Miracles associated with Mary now join with miracles of the Eucharist. Once more, Mary paves the way for her Son.

Across the world, on every habitable continent, people are speaking of special graces linked with that gift above all gifts, that sacrament above all sacraments called the Eucharist.

In this fine book, Fr. Richard Foley, one of the world's most devoted priests, takes us to the most important aspects of the Eucharist and delineates the Virgin Mary's tremendous role with it. He shows that her place is to promote Jesus. He shows that she has come not for her own glory but for that of our Saviour.

Those who have worried that Mary takes attention away from Jesus will now see that the opposite is true. Those who don't understand why she is coming will now see the Light. She has come to attach us more faithfully to Jesus, and she is girding us for difficult times by feeding us the Body of Christ.

Why is Mary so linked with the Eucharist?

Let's consider her role on earth. Let's consider that she had him in her very body for nine months. She enfleshed Jesus and since He *is* the Eucharist she also played a role in enfleshing the Eucharist. In fact the Church even has a special day dedicated to Our Lady of the Blessed Sacrament, and the last one (as of this writing) occurred on May 13.

That's especially interesting because May 13 is a Fatima anniversary, and at Fatima an angel had preceded the Virgin Mary's apparitions and had appeared with a chalice and Host, further linking Mary with the Blessed Sacrament.

Reviewing the Virgin's famous appearances and dissecting her messages, Father Foley shows the intimate and intricate way in which Mary is linked with the Eucharist and how this has indeed been one of her main missions. As he shows, Mary's efforts have been "unceasing" because she knows what most do not: that unless mankind respects Jesus and takes him to heart, we are headed for calamity.

Nothing can substitute for taking part in the Last Supper. No heroics can compare to the simple act of receiving Christ. With the Eucharist, as Father Foley indicates, the way is paved for deliverance. The way is paved for enlightenment. The way is paved for the Truth. It is through the Eucharist—through reception of Communion and prayer before the Blessed Sacrament—that we are illuminated. It is through the Eucharist that we find our path in times that are complex and dark.

I can only hope that this book finds its way to many Catholics, especially priests and those who do not understand Mary's union with her Son. I can only hope that the millions who have been to places like Medjugorje and have seen the miracle of the sun now realize that the "sun" can also be spelled "Son," for it symbolizes the Host, and Jesus is the One behind Mary's authentic apparitions.

Just as we have heard of many apparitions, so now do we hear of many Eucharistic miracles. God is showing us that his Son is truly present in the tabernacle, and we are being flooded with graces.

As Fr. Foley shows, it's Mary's mission that we take those graces and use them to improve our world and purify our souls.

It's her last and fondest wish.

– Michael H. Brown

Chapter One

Two Golden Gifts

When his life was approaching its end, our Saviour left us two precious legacies. First was the Eucharist—the gift of his actual presence abiding really, albeit sacramentally, in our midst. And this gift includes the means not only to produce that presence but to reproduce his Good Friday sacrifice, which takes place in the Mass. Furthermore, the Offerer and Victim of that sacrifice gives himself to us in Holy Communion as food for our souls.

Our Lord's second legacy was the gift of his mother to be our mother also. Thus Mary now beholds in each one of us a beloved child committed to her care by her dying Son; as for St. John, he stood proxy for those human multitudes down the ages who behold in Mary a tender mother and take her into their hearts and homes (cf. Jn. 19:26–27).

Clearly, each of these legacies is pure gold. With regard to the Eucharist, the convert Newman could never get over his glad surprise on seeing the tabernacle in any Catholic church he visited. He referred to this experience as "the blessedness of finding a Treasure Unutterable, the presence of the Eternal Word Incarnate, the Wisdom of the Father."[1]

Several Church Councils and scores of popes down the centuries have exhorted us to treasure this Treasure as it deserves. Pope Leo XIII, for example, hails the Eucharist as "a most divine gift proceeding from the very Heart of the Redeemer."[2]

Any number of saints and mystics have spoken glowing words about the Lord's great gift of the Eucharist. But few can have spoken more glowingly than did St. John Vianney:

> The many wonders of creation can only fill us with astonishment and admiration. But when we speak of the most holy Eucharist we can say that here is to be found the miracle of divine love for us.... Has there been, or will there ever be, a nobler or more magnanimous love than that which He has shown us in the sacrament of love? Must we not say, with the Council of Trent, that his generosity and magnanimity have here exhausted all his treasures? Is there anything on earth or in heaven which can be compared to it?[3]

The Gift of Mary

As for the Redeemer's other precious legacy—Mary—her praises, as she herself predicted, have been sung by her devotees generation after generation. Especially gracious and courtly was the tribute paid the mother of the Eucharistic Christ by St. Anselm of Canterbury; he hailed her as "wonderfully singular and singularly wonderful ... beautiful to behold, lovable to contemplate, delightful to love."[4]

The root reason underlying the eulogies and homages heaped upon Our Lady is that, because she is God's mother, she enjoys in his redemptive plan an altogether exalted status. St. Francis of Sales sees her as the vital link between God's greatness and mankind's wretchedness, playing a leading role in salvation history, besides transcending all creation through being mother of its Creator.

Vatican II affirmed this point:

> Because of her gift of sublime grace, Mary far surpasses all other creatures both in heaven and on earth; thus she occupies a place in the Church which is the highest after Christ and also closest to us.[5]

Two Distinct Realities

As we shall be seeing, Mary and the Eucharistic Saviour are

linked in a dynamic union of redemptive mission and sanctifying action. This arises from what Vatican II referred to as the "indissoluble bond" between Son and mother.[6]

While recognizing this unique bond, our Catholic faith equally recognizes that the God of the Eucharist and his mother, for all their inseparable closeness and vital cooperation in the work of salvation, each stand for a quite separate and distinct reality. And between these two realities there lies a world of difference both in kind and degree.

To begin with the Eucharist. It is the true presence—that is, the living Person—of God the Son, the infinite Creator, the Lord of life and death. Mary, on the other hand, is, like ourselves, a finite human being. Indeed, she was created by her divine Son and also redeemed by him, albeit in that privileged mode we term the Immaculate Conception.

Accordingly we pay the Blessed Sacrament the supreme homage of divine adoration and worship (latria), because He who is there present is the God of heaven and earth, the all-holy Word-made-flesh, our first beginning and our last end.

To his mother, however, we pay that lesser reverence and homage known as hyperdulia; exalted though it is, this remains wholly inferior and subordinate to the divine worship we accord the Son who was born of her.

So in our traditional Catholic devotion to God's mother we certainly do not worship her, as some misinformed critics allege. Neither in belief nor in practice is authentic Marian devotion to be equated with Mariolatry. That is to say, we do not deify God's mother when we contemplate and celebrate what Newman called "the glories of Mary for the sake of her Son." In St. Ambrose's compact formula, Catholics honour Mary as the temple of God, not as the God of the temple.

As will be shown in later chapters, the Eucharist has several different aspects, each profoundly rich in meaning. What will also be seen is that Mariology comprises no less a wealth of theological truths and reflections, all of which relate directly or indirectly to the Eucharist.

As a preliminary step, however, it will help if we briefly refresh our memories as to what we hold concerning the Eucharist and Mary respectively.

The Eucharist in Focus

Pope John Paul II handily summarizes the subject by pointing out that the Eucharist has in fact three distinct dimensions, being "at one and the same time a Sacrifice-sacrament, a Communion-sacrament, and a Presence-sacrament."[7]

Let us consider this trio in turn. The Eucharist is one and the same sacrifice as that of Calvary. Thus, as the Holy Father frequently reminds us, priests stand mystically on Golgotha each time they offer the sacrifice of the Mass.[8]

To put this more technically, the Lord's Good Friday sacrifice is re-presented through the ministry of priests in a sacramental, unbloody manner in the Mass. Thus Christ's redeeming act of immolation as Victim for the world's sins is made present over and over again for the sanctification of the faithful. And they, in turn, are to offer both themselves and the whole of creation to the eternal Father; which they do in, through and with their great High Priest.

Now Christ's redeeming sacrifice presents us with his presence not only as Priest and Victim but as Food. This brings us to the Communion-sacrament, whereby we partake of the living bread that comes down from heaven (cf. Jn. 6:51). Holy Communion increases our union with the God-Man, nourishing our spirits with sanctifying grace. At the same time it increases our charity and, being both sign and instrument of Church unity, builds up our union with all other members of Christ's Mystical Body.

The Sacrament of Presence

Thirdly, the Eucharist is the Presence-sacrament. For it brings into our midst Emmanuel himself—God among us, the Word-made-flesh and now made wafer. This true presence of the God-Man, besides constituting him the Offerer, the Offered and the bread of life, sets him before us and among us as an abiding guest in our tabernacles.

By adoring the Lord truly present there, we effectively deepen the union achieved with him through Holy Communion. In addition, the sanctifying effects of Eucharistic adoration help to prepare us for an ever-worthier reception of sacramental Communion.

"What is our Lord doing in the tabernacle?" St. John Vianney often put this question rhetorically to his congregation; and he would himself duly reply: "He is waiting for us there."

This is absolutely true. The God of the tabernacle longingly awaits our adoration and worship, our love, our thanksgiving for his many gifts, and our reparation for personal sins and those of the world.

Because of that loving presence within it of the Word Incarnate, the tabernacle, to quote Paul VI's *Credo*, is "the living heart of our churches." The heart in question—the Eucharistic Heart of Jesus, the heart of the God-Man—overflows with mercy, goodness and love towards all who approach him.

No one has grasped this consoling truth more clearly than Newman, who addressed the guest in our tabernacles as follows:

> O most sacred, most loving heart of Jesus, thou art concealed in the Holy Eucharist, and thou beatest for us still.... Thou art the heart of the Most High made man.... Thy Sacred Heart is the instrument and organ of thy love. It did beat for us. It yearned for us. It ached for our salvation. It was on fire through zeal, that the glory of God might be manifested in and by us.... In worshipping thee I worship my incarnate God, my Emmanuel.[9]

Mary in Focus

Now for a parallel résumé of what our faith tells us about Mary. Karl Rahner touched the heart of the matter when he wrote:

> The Son of the eternal Father came down to this earth, into our flesh, into our history, and God has assumed for ever this world in the flesh of his Son.

> And all this happened because Mary, by the consent of her faith, became the mother of God.... Her divine motherhood, then, involves Mary at once and as a matter of course in the tremendous, mysterious, shatteringly great drama that is being acted out between the eternal God and this world with its one human race.[10]

Mary's whole underlying meaning, then, is that she is the leading lady in the drama of Jesus, playing a key role in the redemptive mission of the Word Incarnate. Hers is a world of sinless womanhood caught up into divine motherhood and mediation. Thus she embodies in herself an immensity of holiness, intercession and apostolate.

As first step in his salvific plan for fallen mankind, God selected this innocent daughter of Israel to be the mother of his Incarnate Word. By preserving her from contracting the guilt of original sin, He redeemed her antecedently to her conception. Thus immaculately conceived, the full-of-grace handmaid of the Lord was further preserved by God, throughout her entire life, from contracting the least stain of personal sin.

Moreover, so intimately was Mary associated with her Son—the Head of his Mystical Body, the Church—that she now mediates his life of grace to all its members, each of whom she cherishes with a mother's love.

At the end of her earthly sojourn, Mary was taken up body and soul into the glory of heaven. We call this privilege her Assumption; it was conferred both as consequence of, and reward for, her sublime dignity as God's all-holy mother.

Mary is now queen of heaven and mother of the Church. And, as will become clear in subsequent pages, her maternal and grace-mediating role is centred very directly on the Eucharist.

The Two Hearts

John Paul II launched a rich new expression into circulation when he described the relationship between Jesus and Mary as "the admirable alliance of hearts."[11] Right from the beginning, of course, the Church has been well aware of the extra-special understanding, partnership and liaison between the Word-made-flesh and his mother. But the Holy Father's felicitous phrase has happily invested the concept with a new-found freshness and stimulus.

In keeping with Scriptural usage, their hearts symbolize the very selfhood of Jesus and Mary. That is, their physical hearts stand as symbols of their individual selves down to the very core of their being. Mind and will, thoughts and memories, affections and emotions, attitudes and desires—all is encapsulated in the term "heart."

Now what is altogether unique about the heart-symbolism in this context is that the Virgin of Nazareth actually supplied the second Person of the Trinity with his physical heart when He was conceived in her womb. St. Augustine's words here come to mind. The body of Christ, he says, "was created in her whom He had created."[12]

There in Mary's virginal womb the Sacred Heart of Jesus was fashioned beneath her own heart and commenced to beat in unison with it. And there, in that first-ever tabernacle of the real presence, began the admirable alliance that would never end—the covenant of love and collaboration between the Eucharistic Heart of the Redeemer and the Immaculate Heart of Mary.

Throughout Jesus's life, all the way from Nazareth to Calvary, his mother participated wholly and entirely in his redemptive mission. His lifework and hers became fused practically to the point of being identical; so much so, that Mary could say with the poet:

> In his heart my heart is locked,
> And in his life my life.[13]

Now that the Eternal Word's incarnate life and redemptive mission are being continued in the Eucharistic mysteries, Mary's heart and lifework remain inseparably interlocked therein with his.

One Heart Leads to the Other

With regard to the Lord's mission, John Paul II stresses that Mary's special "co-mission" highlights the significance and value of devotion to her Immaculate Heart. For, he explains, "through love of her Son and all humanity she exercises a unique instrumentality in bringing us to him."[14]

Hence devotion to the heart of Mary is the sure road leading to that heart which beats for us in the Blessed Sacrament with a love that is both divine and human. This is the message, we learn from St. Catherine Labouré, that is symbolized by the close proximity of the two hearts on the reverse side of the Miraculous Medal: one is crowned with thorns, the other pierced by a sword.

That visionary's testimony to the alliance of hearts was later echoed by her sister-visionary in Fatima—the amazing little 9-year-old Jacinta Marto (now Venerable). Shortly before her death she urged her cousin, now Sr. Lucia:

> Tell everybody that God grants us all graces through the Immaculate Heart of Mary; that people are to ask her for them; and that the Sacred Heart of Jesus wants the Immaculate Heart of Mary to be venerated at his side.[15]

So clearly does the admirable alliance of hearts illumine the relationship between the Eucharist and the Mother of the Blessed Sacrament, as St. Peter Julian Eymard used to address Our Lady, that it could appropriately serve as a sub-title for this book.

Significantly enough, Pope St. Pius X adjudged Mother of the Blessed Sacrament to be the most theological of all Mary's titles after Mother of God. Readers will find his insight amply verified in the pages that follow.[16]

---

[1] John Henry Cardinal Newman: PAROCHIAL AND PLAIN SERMONS, (London) 1884, VIII, 9

[2] Pope Leo XIII: MIRAE CARITATIS, AAS 34 (1902)

[3] St. John Vianney: SERMONS FOR SUNDAYS AND FEASTS OF THE YEAR: THE HOLY EUCHARIST, (New York) 1901, 176-177

[4] St. Anselm of Canterbury: OPERA OMNIA, Or. 7, 21

[5] Vatican II: LUMEN GENTIUM, 53, 54

---

[6] loc. cit.
[7] Pope John Paul II: REDEMPTOR HOMINIS, 29
[8] Pope John Paul II: HOLY THURSDAY LETTER TO PRIESTS, 1988
[9] John Henry Cardinal Newman: MEDITATIONS AND DEVOTIONS. Introduction by Meriol Trevor, (London) 1964, 86–87
[10] Karl Rahner, S.J.: MARY, MOTHER OF THE LORD. (London) 1963, 56
[11] Pope John Paul II: ANGELUS ADDRESS, 15 September 1985 (Reported in *L'Osserv. Romano*, 23 September 1985)
[12] St. Augustine: SERMON 189, 2, PL 38, 1005
[13] Christina Rossetti: POEMS—NEW AND ENLARGED EDITION: Noble Sisters, (London) 1890
[14] Pope John Paul II: ADDRESS TO INTERNATIONAL SYMPOSIUM, 22 September 1986 (reported in *L'Osserv. Romano*, 26 September 1986)
[15] John M. Haffert: HER OWN WORDS: THE MEMOIRS OF SR. LUCIA (101 Foundation), 1993, 172
[16] Pope St. Pius X: AD DIEM ILLUM, AAS 36 (1903–4)

CHAPTER TWO

Mary and Eucharistic Faith

Faith opens for us a window on the world of the supernatural. This is faith's great gift, its genius. St. Augustine often spoke of "the eyes of faith."[1] For faith is essentially vision of a kind. It *sees*. And what faith sees, howsoever dimly and fitfully, is the kingdom of God. Our faith-experience of that unseen kingdom's mysteries and splendours has been memorably expressed by Francis Thompson:

> O world invisible, we view thee.
> O world intangible, we touch thee.
> O world unknowable, we know thee.
> Inapprehensible, we clutch thee.[2]

It is at Baptism that the vision of faith is given to us along with hope and charity, the other two so-called theological virtues. Thus equipped with the eyes of faith, we are enabled, once we attain the use of reason, to behold that vast supernatural panorama which is the kingdom of God.

The three divine Persons feature primarily, of course, within faith's purview. And we can focus our gaze as we please on other persons, such as the queen of heaven, or the innumerable host of spirits both angelic and human, or the souls in purgatory. And, too, faith-vision can focus on holy *things* in the Communion of Saints besides on holy persons—things like credal truths, the mystery of the Church, the sacred Scriptures, the sacraments.

Eucharistic Faith

What makes the Eucharist different from other sacraments is that it presents us, *in person*, with their Author. While faith in general sees the kingdom of God, the God of the kingdom himself comes immediately into view when faith focuses on the Eucharist. For Emmanuel's very Self is really and truly present in the consecrated elements, albeit in sacramental form.

"We have him before our eyes," proclaims Gerard Manley Hopkins, "masked in the sacred Host."[3] The identical truth is expressed in St. Thomas's great Benediction hymn:

> Faith our outward sense befriending,
> Makes the inward vision clear.

What our inward vision beholds in the Blessed Sacrament is the actual, factual, physical, substantial, integral Real Presence of him whom St. Augustine often calls the Man-God, complete with his glorified humanity and divinity. No one has grasped this tremendous truth more firmly than Newman. He declares:

> Do we not believe in a Presence in the sacred tabernacle, not as a form of words or as a notion, but as an object as real as we are?[4]

Because of its exalted status and dignity, the Blessed Sacrament is traditionally styled *the* mystery of faith, that is, the mystery of faith *par excellence*. For it out-faiths all other sacraments, inasmuch as each of them is limited to producing some*thing* holy and sanctifying, whereas the Eucharist presents us with Some*one*—He who is the fountain of all holiness besides being faith's Giver and Rewarder (cf. Heb. 12:2).

Where Faith Was Born

Now to see how all this links up with Mary. The roots of our faith—including our Eucharistic faith—go directly back to her role in the Annunciation episode. That was in itself a private revelation, preliminary to and preparatory for the public one to be inaugurated by the Messiah-Revealer.

Mary made a supreme act of faith and obedience, thereby mediating and in a sense inaugurating the Incarnation with its manifold follow-on mysteries, pre-eminently the Eucharist. The scenario of that opening scene in the drama of Jesus is familiar to us from the gospel. The Word was made flesh in Mary's virginal womb when she consented to God's proposal that she should be the mother of the Messiah-Redeemer.

Mary's consent marked the dramatic moment when the Second Person of the Trinity began his incarnate life among us. Nor did his incarnate presence cease when He left this world. For his promise to remain with us all days has ever since been fulfilled quite literally in his ongoing role as our Eucharistic Emmanuel—the sacrament containing the selfsame humanity as was fashioned in the Virgin's womb.

Now the whole point about the Annunciation is that Mary's faith functioned as the very hinge upon which depended the entire course of Christian salvation history, including the major part to be played therein by the Eucharist. Our Lady's consent to God's initiative was the indispensable condition for his redemptive plan to go into operation.

Mary's Unique Faith

We can only wonder at the sheer strength, daring, and utter trust, let alone the momentous consequences, of Mary's act of belief and acceptance. Upon that act, as the Holy Father said in a homily at Lourdes, depended nothing less than the redemption of the world.[5] Or in Rahner's words: "Mary's voice became the voice of all mankind."[6]

To gauge the sheer magnitude of Mary's faith, we should recall that there was absolutely no precedent in the Old Testament for such a prodigy: namely, a virgin conceiving a son, let alone a Messianic one. Nonetheless Mary consented to God's plan, trusting him without hesitation or compromise. It was on her part a quantum leap of blind, heroic faith, obedient and trusting, into the arms of divine providence.

"Blessed art thou for thy believing!" (Lk. 1:45). Elizabeth's words to Our Lady can now also be applied in due measure to ourselves, since we, too, have been blessed to high heaven through the mega-faith of the Lord's handmaid.

A New Covenant was inaugurated when Mary, the Virgin of Nazareth, became the Woman of Faith and the New Eve—in direct antithesis to the disobedience and disbelief of Adam's partner. And, as St. Thomas comments, Mary contracted a spiritual marriage between the human race, there represented by herself, and the Son of God.[7]

The Mother of Our Faith

> Christ is truth, Christ is flesh:
> Christ-truth in the mind of Mary,
> Christ-flesh in the womb of Mary.[8]

In this text from one of his sermons, St. Augustine voiced a theme common among the Church Fathers—those theological giants of the early Christian centuries. Here the central idea is that Mary's acceptance of God's word in her mind was the indispensable preliminary to the conception of his Word in her womb.

A further leading idea among the Fathers is that we believers are conceived as God's children *through Mary's faith*. That is to say, Nazareth became at the Annunciation the Bethlehem, so to call it, of our Christian belief. Thus the Virgin's prodigious act of believing was not only exemplary in our regard but primordial, seminal, initiating, germinative, generating, quasi-creative. This became standard teaching among Christian writers, as exemplified in the following text:

> Through Mary, Christ is our brother. Everything that the brother means to us is from the mother, because that flesh is our flesh and that faith—your faith, O Mary—is our faith.[9]

Mary and Eucharistic Faith

The maternal heart of Mary ardently desires to strengthen and encourage the faith engendered in us through her Yes at Nazareth. This theme is especially dear to Pope John Paul II:

> For every Christian, for every human being, Mary is the one who first believed, and precisely with her faith as spouse and mother she wishes to act upon all those who entrust themselves to her as her children.... The more her children persevere and progress in this attitude, the nearer Mary leads them to the unsearchable riches of Christ.[10]

These "unsearchable riches of Christ" are totally present in the Eucharist. Indeed, they are literally *embodied* there. For beneath the Eucharist's sacramental veils is the living fruit of Mary's womb. And our faith in his presence there is, in turn, the fruit of Mary's shining faith which in the first place set the drama of redemption on course.

Cana and the Eucharist

At Nazareth, Mary's faith was instrumental in bringing us the God-Man as such. At Cana, on the other hand, her faith brought him to public notice as the Messiah displaying miraculous power—the same power that would later transform bread and wine into the Eucharistic gift.

The gospel account of the Cana episode (cf. Jn. 2:1–11) hinges on the social crisis experienced by a bridal couple at their wedding celebration. The supply of wine had run out. And this was immediately noticed by Our Lady. She appealed to Jesus to intervene; initially, however, He demurred, aware that "his hour"—that is, the appointed time for making his public debut as the Messiah—had not yet come.

Yet Mary's confidence in Jesus's power and goodness remained unshaken. She exhorted the chief steward to carry out whatever instructions her Son would give. And we know the sequel: six large containers of water were transmuted by Our Lord into wine—to the vast relief of their hosts, not to forget the undying astonishment of that chief steward and his staff.

Towards the Eucharistic Banquet

The Cana gospel abounds in lessons and symbolisms. To begin with, it shows the efficacy of Mary's intercession, which actually brought about an advancement of the date when Christ's messianic ministry would commence.

Furthermore, Mary already possessed that faith which our Lord purposed to awaken in his disciples precisely through this prodigy. The gospel text makes this quite clear:

> So in Cana of Galilee Jesus began his miracles and made known the glory that was his, so that his disciples learned to believe in him.[11]

In launching her Son so dramatically on his public ministry, Mary effectively raised the Cana celebration to the status of a messianic banquet—that is, a figure of the joys of the long-prophesied messianic kingdom in which there would be an abundance of wine supplied by the Messiah himself (cf. Is. 25:6). And the Messiah surely had this same thought in mind when He said on a later occasion: "The kingdom of heaven is to be compared to a king who made a marriage-feast for his son" (Mt. 22:2–14).

Moreover, through the transformation of water into wine, the Cana messianic banquet prefigured a momentous messianic banquet still to come—the Last Supper. And it, in turn, would be elevated into a Eucharistic banquet when the Messiah changed the bread and wine into his body and blood.

Nor was that all. The Eucharistic banquet, too, was to have a higher orientation: namely, to the Messiah's heavenly banquet. For the cup which He shared with his disciples, Jesus declared, was a symbol and pledge of what He would share with them beyond this world—the definitive and everlasting messianic banquet in the glory of the Father's kingdom (cf. Mt. 26:29; Lk. 22:16, 18).

This explains why in the Eucharistic liturgy there occur frequent reminders and anticipations of that heavenly banquet awaiting us as faith's goal and reward.

Cana and Priesthood

Mary's leading role in the Cana drama is further evident in what we saw earlier: the effect it produced on Christ's future apostles. They recognized the prodigy as a sign of his divine nature and so came to believe in him.

The future apostles' new-found faith marked a momentous development in the gospel story. And the faith generated in them at Cana would be reinforced in the days to come by many further miracles performed by their Master. Prominent among these was the feeding of the multitude on just a handful of loaves.

In fact, it was precisely these miracles featuring the transformation of water into wine and the multiplication of bread that prefigured the miracle of the Eucharist. This took place at the Last Supper, where the Lord's apostles received his body and blood transubstantiated by him from bread and wine.

Also at the Last Supper, the Master of the Apostles conferred on them a share in his own priesthood, thus empowering them to re-offer his sacrificial death for the life and sanctification of the world. "Do this," He said, "in memory of me" (Lk. 22:19).

The Last Supper was in effect the first of countless ordination ceremonies throughout the centuries to come. Thus by means of the ordained priesthood the Eucharistic mysteries of Christ's loving presence and life-giving sacrifice are perpetuated. Thus, too, those multitudes for whom He died—uncounted multitudes spread across the five continents in every age to come—partake of the messianic banquet by eating the bread of life and drinking the cup of salvation.

For these prodigious gifts, then, we have to thank not only our Eucharistic Lord but the mother of the Eucharist—Our Lady of Cana. For it was her wonderful faith, her tender solicitude, and her confident intercession that set in motion the sequence of messianic banquets leading to the Eucharist and culminating in the feast of eternal life.

Mary's Pilgrimage of Faith

"Mary advanced on her pilgrimage of faith."[12] Thus did Vatican

II remind us that Mary, like ourselves, was a "pilgrim and stranger" in this world and that she "walked by faith" (cf. Heb. 11:13; 2 Cor. 5:7).

Mary's was a very privileged and high-grade faith, of course, consistent with her role as the sinlessly conceived virgin chosen to be mother of the Eternal Word. Moreover, her faith would surely have received powerful illuminations at certain key points in her life.

What sort of faith-vision, we may wonder, did Our Lady enjoy at the time she said Yes to the will of God as made known by the archangel? Hers was the faith of a devout daughter of Israel. Now Israel, committed as it was to the kingdom of God and his covenant, cherished the sacred Scriptures and entertained a lively expectation of the promised Messiah. All in all, however, the scope of Israel's faith, focused as it was on Old Testament revelation, was considerably less extensive in its content than the Christian dispensation that succeeded it.

Mary's Knowledge

The principal question to arise is: did Mary know right from the start that her Offspring was the Son of God? Certainly the dialogue between her and the archangel scarcely leaves room for doubt that she realized her Son was divine. St. Thomas takes this for granted, affirming, as we noted earlier, that Mary contracted a spiritual marriage between God's Son and the human race, there represented by herself.

Pope St. Leo the Great voiced the virtually unanimous verdict of patristic authors when he wrote:

> A royal virgin of the race of David is chosen who would become pregnant with a sacred Offspring, and would conceive her divine and human Offspring in her mind before doing so in her body.[13]

As for St. Bernard, he declares on several occasions that it was the eternal Son of the Father whom Mary knowingly conceived and mothered. Pope St. Pius X echoes this, stating explicitly that the Virgin was fully conscious from the outset that in her womb had taken place the mystery of the Incarnation—"the beginning and foundation of faith."[14]

While some modern exegetes may have reservations as to whether the Virgin of the Annunciation realized her Son was the Eternal Word of the Father, most authorities agree that the gospel text itself places the matter beyond reasonable doubt.

Yet this does not rule out that Mary's faith in her Son's divinity co-existed with certain obscurities, and that as time went by she came to grasp more and more clearly the momentous implications of the secret she cherished. This growth in her understanding of the divine truth thus prefigured the so-called development of doctrine that the Church would experience with the passage of time.

Mary the Sole Believer

It is clear that Mary alone at the Cana marriage-feast believed in her Son's divine nature. And it was precisely this faith that prompted her to approach him, implicitly invoking his divine power to help the bridal couple out of their predicament. The sequel to the ensuing miracle was that the Lord's disciples came to share the faith in Christ's divinity that his mother had held from the beginning.

It was again Mary, and she alone, who continued to believe in her Son's divinity during the bitter hours of his Passion. There is a consensus about this among medieval theologians. St. Thomas, for example, was convinced that Mary's faith, and hers alone, remained entirely secure. St. Bonaventure was quite explicit, even going on to explain that this is why the Church holds special devotions on Holy Saturday in honour of Our Lady of Sorrows.

> The Virgin Mary always persisted in the faith.... While the disciples did not believe and doubted, she was the one in whom the faith of the Church remained solid and unshaken.[15]

Mary's Eucharistic Experience

After the Lord's Ascension into heaven and the coming of the Holy Spirit at Pentecost, the small Christian community, including the mother of Jesus, maintained the closest union with him through the Eucharistic mysteries, which they designated "the breaking of bread" (cf. Acts 2:42, 46; Lk. 24:35).

Thus Our Lady's faith now took on, like our own, a Eucharistic mode. As St. Peter Julian Eymard says:

> Mary found again in the adorable Host the adorable fruit of her womb ... and began in the Cenacle her new maternity at the feet of Jesus in the Eucharist.[16]

Along with her fellow-worshippers Mary would co-offer herself in union with the sacrificial Victim when the officiating priest spoke the words of consecration over the bread and wine. And, again like the others, she would receive the sacred body of Jesus in Holy Communion.

It is impossible to conceive how pure, deep and tender must have been Mary's love for her Son now concealed, yet truly and integrally present, under their sacramental forms.

Each time his Calvary sacrifice was renewed, the Mother of Sorrows re-lived the dark hours of Good Friday and once again offered co-redemptively to the Father the spiritual agony she had endured. And, every occasion she received the Lord's living self in Holy Communion, it was for her maternal heart a joy beyond all telling.

Thus Mary's faith came to focus principally on the Eucharistic mysteries and to feast on them. In and through this sacrament her soul daily magnified that same Lord whose humanity had been formed in her womb. In and through this sacrament her spirit rejoiced in God her Saviour. And, gazing upon his abiding presence in the consecrated species, she worshipped him in spirit and in truth, just as she had done all the way from crib to cross.

"Better than any other creature, angelic or human," St. Peter Julian Eymard remarks, "Mary comprehended the immensity of the Eucharistic gift."[17] Earlier she had witnessed that gift's twin prefigurations in the multiplication of loaves and the changing of water into wine. Furthermore, her sensitive faith-vision enabled her to perceive most keenly in this sacrament the God-Man's consuming love—for herself in the first place, and for the world-wide human family He had in his dying moments entrusted to her maternal care.

Mary Then and Now

Having seen something of Our Lady's own first-hand experience as a pilgrim of faith in general and of Eucharistic faith in particular, we can accept her all the more confidently as our guide and inspiration with regard to the Blessed Sacrament. She will lead us to make this treasure, as did St. Ignatius, "the support and companion of our pilgrimage."

We can be confident that the mother of the Eucharist will fire us with something of her own zeal for God's kingdom in ourselves and in others. For, as Karl Rahner reminds us, we sons and daughters of Mary have been filled, as she was to an eminent degree, with choice gifts from heaven precisely so that we may more effectively work to share them with others. Rahner further points out:

> We too are anointed, hallowed, filled with the light and life of God. We too have been sent by him, so that we too may carry the light of faith and the flame of love, through this world's darkness, to the place where we belong, in his eternal radiance.[18]

Our next step will be to examine how intimately associated is the mother of the Eucharist with its awesome central mystery—her Son's redeeming death ritually and repeatedly re-offered, until He comes again, on our altars.

---

[1] St. Augustine: ENARR. IN PS. 146:19, PL 37, 1897

[2] Francis Thompson: POEMS: THE KINGDOM OF GOD, (London) 1909

[3] Gerard Manley Hopkins: POEMS AND PROSE. Selected by W. H. Gardner, (Penguin) 1966, 136

[4] John Henry Cardinal Newman: DIFFICULTIES OF ANGLICANS, (London) 1850, 388
[5] Pope John Paul II: LOURDES HOMILY IN AUGUST 1983 (Reported *in L'Osserv. Romano*, 5 September 1983)
[6] Karl Rahner,S.J.: MARY, MOTHER OF THE LORD, (London) 1963, 104
[7] St. Thomas Aquinas: SUMMA THEOLOGICA, Pars 3, q. 30, a. I
[8] St. Augustine: SERMO 25, 7, PL 46, 938
[9] Rupert of Deutz: PL 170, 404D–405A
[10] Pope John Paul II: REDEMPTORIS MATER, 46
[11] JOHN 2:11
[12] Vatican II: LUMEN GENTIUM, 58
[13] Pope St. Leo the Great: SERMO 21, PL 54, 191
[14] Pope St. Pius X: AD DIEM ILLUM, AAS 36 (1903–4)
[15] St. Bonaventure: IN 3 SENT. D. 111
[16] St. Peter Julian Eymard: IN THE LIGHT OF THE MONSTRANCE. Edited by Charles DeKeyser, S.S.S., (Cleveland) 1947
[17] St. Peter Julian Eymard: loc. cit.
[18] Karl Rahner, S.J.: MARY, MOTHER OF THE LORD, (London) 1963, 49

CHAPTER THREE

Mary and the Mass

Jesus of Nazareth, as Chesterton noted, is the only man ever to come into this world with the express purpose of dying. Death was his longed-for quest and goal, the coveted crown and fulfilment of his earthly mission. For He came as our Redeemer, and his redemptive sacrifice was to bring about atonement between God and sinful humanity.

No one was more sensitively aware of the Redeemer's sacrificial destiny than his mother. Nor was anyone closer than she to its dramatic final scene on Good Friday. Standing at the foot of the cross, Mary watched her Son bleeding from a thousand wounds before breathing his last. And her mother's heart was caught up into the most profound compassion with those sufferings and death that wrought our salvation.

Right from the outset the mother of the Word Incarnate had been closely associated with his life and lifework as Saviour of mankind. But it was her compassion with his redemptive sacrifice that marked the high point of the lifelong alliance between his heart and her own. As a distinguished disciple of St. Bernard said about this:

> There were really two altars on Calvary. One was in Mary's heart, the other in Christ's body. He sacrificed his flesh, Mary her soul.[1]

Mary's Spiritual Co-Sacrifice

Indeed, Our Lady's spiritual co-sacrifice in union with her Son's amounted to the closest-possible cooperation, in a subordinately co-redemptive way, with the Calvary sacrifice. In recognition of this the Redeemer appointed her mother of the redeemed; thus she now plays a central role in distributing among her children the divine gifts and graces won for us by the atoning death of Jesus.

Now the greatest of all God's gifts and graces is unquestionably the Eucharist—the sacrament that is also a sacrifice. And the Eucharist enjoys this paramount status because it literally reproduces, re-presents, the Calvary sacrifice in the ritual form we call the Mass.

Pope Pius XII's simple formula sums things up concisely. "Christ," he says, "does on our altars what he did on the Cross."[2] Hence, as St. John Vianney often told his parishioners, the Mass virtually turns every day into Good Friday. Thomas à Kempis exhorts us in similar vein:

> When you assist at Mass, it should appear to you as new and as great as if, at the time, you were actually looking at Christ suffering and dying for mankind's salvation.[3]

United with Our High Priest

Given what Vatican II calls the "indissoluble bond" uniting Mary and her divine Son,[4] it follows that, as mother of the Eucharistic Jesus, she now remains just as closely united with his sacramental sacrifice as with its prototype on Golgotha. In other words, the Virgin is present at every Mass with its High Priest and Victim, re-offering him—and herself along with him—to the Eternal Father, renewing her maternal compassion, and exercising her universal intercession.

This explains why the mother of the faithful so earnestly desires that we attend Mass frequently and fervently. For thereby we become united in the most sanctifying way possible with him who, through the ministry of his ordained priests, makes present before us and for our sakes, in Pope Leo XIII's phrase, "the memorial of his measureless love for mankind."[5]

To this end our great High Priest has empowered his faithful to co-offer themselves in the Mass—with him, through him and in him—to the Father. And this privileged empowerment flows from the "royal priesthood" that the Lord's followers receive through being consecrated to him in Baptism (cf. 1 Pet. 2:9).

Nor is it only themselves that the faithful are to offer to God. All material creation must likewise be lifted up with the Host in thanksgiving and praise to its Creator. And the mother of our Creator joins the faithful in co-offering this good earth, together with its manifold fruits and benefits, to him who made them for our use, enjoyment and service.

Mother of Our High Priest

Having seen in brief outline some of the main aspects of Mary's relationship to the redemptive sacrifice, let us now look at them a little more closely. We start with the mystery of Mary's maternal role in preparing the way for the sacrifice of the cross.

To begin with, it was in her virginal womb that the Eternal Word received from the Holy Spirit his humanity and the priestly anointing which constituted him "a priest for ever" (Ps. 110:4). And that same Holy Spirit not only made Mary's flesh into a tabernacle of God's presence but consecrated her heart as an altar of sacrifice. For this true daughter of Israel knew from the Scriptures, notably the prophecy of Isaiah (ch. 51), that her Messiah-Son—her very own flesh and blood—was destined one day to suffer and die for his people.

This sombre prospect became all too painfully definite and clear on the day Mary presented the Infant Jesus in the temple (cf. Lk. 2:22–35). Her soul, declared the ancient Simeon prophetically, was to be pierced by a sword—the sword that time-future would hold sheathed in its scabbard all those years till the dark hours of the Passion.

St. Bernard, like many others before and after, saw in that mystery of the Presentation a foreshadowing of Mary's role on Good Friday. This prompted him to pray:

> Sacrosanct Virgin, offer your Son and present the fruit of your womb to the Lord. For our reconcilia-

> tion with all, offer the heavenly Victim pleasing to God.[6]

Indeed, the Messiah's mother made that offering a constant practice from his infancy onwards. As Pope St. Pius X saw so clearly, Mary brought Jesus up from his earliest years with the prime motive of preparing him for the redemptive role He would later consummate through his bitter sufferings and death.[7]

Mary and the Cross-Sacrifice

Vatican II has supplied us with a key text:

> The Blessed Virgin advanced on her pilgrimage of faith and faithfully persevered in her union with her Son unto the cross. There she stood, in keeping with the divine plan, enduring with her only-begotten Son the intensity of his suffering, joining herself with his sacrifice in her mother's heart, and lovingly consenting to the immolation of this Victim born of her.... In a wholly singular way Mary cooperated in the work of the Saviour.[8]

In offering her Son to the Father, Mary also made what is often referred to as the holocaust of her maternal rights and motherly love. Through her deep compassion and close association with the suffering Saviour, the mother of our Head according to the flesh became the mother according to the spirit of all members of his Mystical Body.

For the same reasons, Mary participated in an altogether special and privileged way in the priesthood of her Son as He offered himself in atonement for the world's sins. For she co-offered her own spiritual grief along with his torments. Already at the Annunciation she had been endowed with what has been described as a "priestly maternity"—precisely because, as mother of the great High Priest, she would wholeheartedly consent to offer him to God and, at the same time, be spiritually co-offered with him and for him.

The Vespers hymn for Our Lady of Sorrows helps us to

picture that scene:

> Under the world-redeeming rood
> The most afflicted mother stood;
> Her Son, upon its altar laid,
> The eternal expiation made.

Because a priest is essentially someone who offers sacrifices to God, Mary merited that title in a most exalted way. But her priesthood is of a wholly different kind from that which derives from the sacrament of Orders; nor, as we shall presently see, is Mary's priesthood identical at all points with the so-called priesthood of the faithful.

Just as the Son she conceived was constituted a priest through the hypostatic union—that is, the fusion of his humanity with the Second Person of the Trinity—the Virgin's whole maternal being, destiny and role were consecrated by the Holy Spirit to a priest-like life of selfless self-offering, which reached its climax at the foot of the cross.

Furthermore, at the foot of the cross the merits of Mary's total union of mind and heart with the crucified Christ were integrated by him into his own redemptive merits. Thus she was privileged to participate in them wholly and completely.

Thus, too, Mary's spiritual and maternal priesthood assumed a universal dimension and outreach. For, as mother of the Mystical Body, she now mediates to us in their entirety the redemptive gifts won at such cost by its Head. We accordingly honour her with the title Mediatrix of All Graces.

Cross and Altar

"The sacrifice of the Cross is sacramentally realized on our altars." This formula in Pope Paul VI's *Credo* sums up the whole underlying mystery of the Mass. From earliest times the Church has taught that the Christ of the Eucharistic sacrifice is identical with the Christ of history, the Christ who suffered under Pontius Pilate.

Moreover, between the cross-sacrifice and the altar-sacrifice there is a substantial and numerical identity. The selfsame High Priest offers the selfsame Victim, only the mode of offering being different.

On Calvary the Word-made-flesh was immolated brutally and bloodily in a supreme act of self-sacrifice for the world's redemption. But his sacrifice was not simply an historical event like any other, an event which, though momentous in itself, was inevitably doomed, like all historical events as such, to be consigned forever to the chronicles of the past.

On the contrary, that altogether special historical event—Christ's Calvary-sacrifice—becomes living and alive, perennial, fully contemporary with his faithful in every generation. And it does so in and through the sacrifice of the altar. By this means, as Pope John Paul II frequently reminds us, the blood-stained Calvary-sacrifice is actualized—that is, its very reality is reproduced, re-done, re-presented—in the sacramental form we call the Mass.[9]

What this signifies, then, is that Mass perpetuates the sacrifice of the cross. They are one and the same sacrifice, vested with the Saviour's identical sacrificial dispositions and actions.

What is further signified is that the Eucharistic mystery bursts the bonds of time and space, allowing us, the faithful, to co-participate mystically in the saving act of our redemption performed those many centuries ago. The sacred drama of Good Friday is re-performed in our midst for the sanctification of our sinful selves.

Perpetuating the Sacrifice

An apparent problem may seem to arise as to how we are to reconcile the all-sufficiency of the Calvary-sacrifice with the practice of perpetuating it in the Mass. Pius XII has clearly formulated the solution:

> If individual sinners are to be purified in the blood of the Lamb, Christians themselves must cooperate. Although Christ, universally speaking, has reconciled the whole human race to the Father by his death, yet he has willed that all men should come

> and be brought to his cross, especially by means of the sacraments and the Mass, and so take possession of the fruits which through the cross He has won for them.... Among the instruments for distributing to believers the merits that flow from the cross of the divine Redeemer, the august sacrifice of the altar is pre-eminent.[10]

As a subsequent chapter will explain, the Mass ritual, in addition to being a sacrifice, is a banquet, a paschal meal in which we receive the Lord's body and blood as Holy Communion. And hereby we participate in, and as it were re-live, the mystery of the Last Supper. For it was there that the Eucharist was instituted and Holy Communion distributed for the first time.

First and foremost, however, the Mass is a sacrifice—one and the same as the real-life sacrifice witnessed by Our Lady on Good Friday. The separate words of consecration over the bread and wine both symbolize and re-present the separation in death of the divine Victim's body and blood. And that death is made present, shown forth on the altar, each time we "break the bread and drink the cup" of the Eucharist (cf. 1 Cor. 11:26).

Richard Crashaw's verse captures something of the sanctifying and vivifying effect of the Eucharistic sacrifice:

> So from his living and life-giving death
> My dying life may draw a new and never-fleeting
> breath.[11]

Mary Also Renews Her Sacrifice

Now to show how the mother of God features just as vitally and integrally in the altar-sacrifice as she did in its Calvary prototype. Following Fr. René Laurentin's suggestion, let us recall that the part Mary now plays in the mysteries of the Blessed Sacrament corresponds exactly to her role during the Lord's mortal days.[12] And, in turn, the part she plays in his Eucharistic sacrifice corresponds exactly to her role in the sacrifice of the cross.

Many eminent authorities, including St. Bonaventure and St. John Eudes, emphasize that in the Mass the queen of heaven, in virtue of her unique participation in the cross-sacrifice, again unites her co-offering both of the adorable Victim and of her own maternal compassion and grief. St. Peter Julian Eymard goes on to say that every grace we receive through the Eucharistic sacrifice is mediated to us by its mystical co-offerer and co-victim, whom he duly titled Our Lady of the Blessed Sacrament.[13]

This mystery of Mary's co-presence and cooperation in the Mass finds a frequent echo in Pope John Paul II. For example:

> Every Mass is a memorial of that one sacrifice and that passover which restored life to the world. Every Mass puts us into intimate communion with her, the mother, whose sacrifice "becomes present" just as the sacrifice of her Son "becomes present" at the words of consecration.... At the root of the Eucharist is the virginal and maternal life of Mary.[14]

Mary's Presence in the Mass

The place of honour accorded to Mary in the Eucharistic liturgy, especially the Canons, reflects how highly the Church values her vital status and function in the sacred mysteries.

Interestingly enough, a good many saints and mystics in every age have testified to their own personal awareness of the mother of God's presence during Mass. Their testimonies throw much light on the issues we are considering in this chapter. And they further serve to stimulate our personal faith and devotion towards the Eucharist.

Four Instances of Mary's Presence

Here follow four such testimonies. They come respectively from St. Ignatius Loyola, Blessed Faustina Kowalska, Padre Pio, and Fr. Stefano Gobbi.

1. **St. Ignatius Loyola**: *Spiritual Diary, Friday, 15 February 1544: Feast of the Presentation*[15]

   During much of this time—before, during and after

Mass—I felt and saw clearly that Our Lady was very propitious, pleading before the Father. Indeed, during the prayers to the Father and the Son, and at his consecration, I could not but feel and see her, as though she were part or rather portal of the great grace that I could feel in my spirit. [At the consecration she showed that her own flesh was in that of her Son], with so many intuitions that they could not be written.

(The editors refer thus to the bracketed phrase: "The brackets are St. Ignatius', probably underlining the importance of this intuition.")

2. **Blessed Faustina Kowalska**: *Spiritual Diary, 8 December, Feast of the Immaculate Conception*[16]

From early morning I felt the nearness of the Blessed Mother. During Holy Mass I saw her, so lovely and so beautiful that I have no words to express even a small part of this beauty. She was all in white, with a blue sash around her waist. Her cloak was also blue, and there was a crown on her head. Marvellous light streamed forth from her whole figure.

She said, "I am the queen of heaven and earth, but especially the mother of your Congregation." She pressed me to her heart and said, "I feel constant compassion for you." I felt the force of her Immaculate Heart which was communicated to my soul. Now I understand why I have been preparing for this feast for two months and have been looking forward to it with such yearning.

3. **Padre Pio**: *(from a letter,*[17] *as told to Padre Alberto D'Apolito in an interview*[18]*)*

Padre Pio: What great care Our Lady took to accompany me to the altar this morning! It seemed to me that she had nothing else to think about except myself as she filled my whole heart with sentiments of holy love.

Padre D'Apolito: Was the Madonna present at your Mass?

Padre Pio: Yes, she placed herself to the side. But I could see her. What joy! What paradise!

Padre D'Apolito: Has she attended your Mass only once, or is she always present?

Padre Pio: How can the mother of Jesus, present at the foot of the cross on Calvary, who offered her Son as Victim for the salvation of souls, be absent at the mystical Calvary of the altar?

Padre D'Apolito: Is Our Lady present at all Masses being celebrated in the world?

Padre Pio: Yes.

Padre D'Apolito: Do the angels also attend?

Padre Pio: The whole celestial court is present.

Padre D'Apolito concluded the above interview with this comment: "That was why Mass was both Calvary and paradise for Padre Pio."

4. **Fr. Stefano Gobbi**: *Our Lady's message on Good Friday, 20 April 1984*[19]

Good Friday is repeated when Jesus immolates himself for you, though in an unbloody manner, in the sacrifice of the Holy Mass. The supreme gift of this day is mystically renewed for you.

But, close to Jesus who immolates himself, the sorrowful oblation of your mother is also repeated. She is always present, close to every altar upon which Mass is celebrated, just as she was present during that long and sorrowful Good Friday.

Priesthood of the Faithful

> When Mary is preached and venerated, she summons the faithful to her Son and his sacrifice and to love for the Father.... They are invited and led to offer themselves, their work and all creation with Christ.[20]

In these words, Vatican II points out that the mother of the Mass-Victim mobilizes and encourages us to co-offer with him his redeeming sacrifice made present on the altar—as well as to offer him our own selves and the world we live in. We are able to stand before God as offerers by virtue of our baptismal status, which anoints us as members of her Son's Mystical Body. Because, like its Head, this worldwide mystical reality is essentially priestly, so, too, by participation are we its members.

Essentially, therefore, we are a sacerdotal corps. For our entire being has been consecrated to God through Baptism and thereby sealed with a special character designating us, now and forever, as sharers in Christ's priesthood. Hence St. Peter could exhort his Christian readers: "You are a chosen race, a royal priesthood, a consecrated nation" (1 Pet. 2:9).

Their baptismal priesthood entitles and enables the faithful to co-offer, together with the celebrant, the Christ of the altar-sacrifice to the Father. Hence at the Offertory the celebrant speaks of "my sacrifice and yours."

Lay people are not empowered, however, to co-consecrate the bread and wine along with the celebrant. This function belongs exclusively to those who have received, through the sacrament of Orders, that fuller participation in Christ's priesthood which is variously termed official, ministerial, hierarchical.

As Mary stood at the foot of the cross, so are the faithful present at the foot of the altar. But, as we have seen, they co-offer the identical sacrifice of the identical Victim through the hands of the identical High Priest. His mother also unites herself with the whole Church in each and every sacramental oblation of the Redeemer.

Besides offering their Redeemer to God in the Mass, the faithful likewise make a self-offering. As St. Augustine put it, we ourselves are laid on the altar as an oblation.

Our Cosmic Offering

In addition, the faithful offer to the Lord of all creation that manifold of good things here represented by the bread and wine. What this signifies is that we place on the paten, to be offered along with the Eucharistic Christ and our own unworthy selves, the universe itself, nothing and nobody excepted. In the words of Vatican II: "The laity consecrate the world to God."[21]

These considerations bring home to us the vast perspectives of the Eucharistic sacrifice. And we present it to God, complete with its cosmic dimensions, through the hands of "the Queen of the Cosmos and of each of us singly," as St. Catherine Labouré liked to style the Blessed Virgin.

Our Personal Sacrifices

As the foregoing material indicates, the oblation that we make of the divine Victim at Mass should be accompanied by the offering of ourselves as co-victims—following the example of the Mother of Sorrows at the Good Friday sacrifice. But it is also *apart from the Mass* that an element of self-immolation forms an integral part of the Christian vocation. As St. Peter instructs us, those who share in the holy priesthood of baptism are called "to offer spiritual sacrifices acceptable to God through Jesus Christ" (1 Pet. 2:5).

St. Paul presribes much the same programme. We are to present our bodies "as a sacrifice, living, holy, pleasing to God" (Rom. 12:1). And he sets before us as an example his own practice of offering his sufferings on behalf of his fellow-men, thereby "filling up what is wanting in the sufferings of Christ, for his body which is the Church" (Col. 1:24).

Here we are in the area of "spiritual priesthood," as St.

Thomas calls the offering of spiritual sacrifices to God. In a spiritual sense, he says, we function as priests when we make the "mystical sacrifice" of ourselves as living hosts or victims.[22]

This element of self-sacrifice and victimhood in union with Christ is a vital expression of our status, conferred through the baptismal priesthood, as living temples of the Trinity (cf. 1 Cor. 3:16). Other expressions of our sacred temple-status can take the form of praise, thanksgiving and intercession. In these various ways, which correspond to and express our varying human circumstances and needs, we offer due worship to God in the temple of our selfhood.

Mary and Victim-Souls

Like every form of sacrifice, human self-sacrifice is fundamentally offered to God in reparation for sins—one's own sins to begin with. When offered for others, self-sacrifice also becomes the prayer of intercession for the souls of others.

This victim-soul principle is embodied in the so-called Morning Offering, one common version of which runs:

> O Eucharistic Heart of Jesus, through the most pure heart of Mary I offer you every thought, word, deed and suffering of this day, in union with the intentions of your divine heart and of our Holy Father the Pope.

Some chosen souls are called to practise victimhood to a heroic degree. Here a galaxy of names comes to mind. These are those souls whose passionate love of God and ardent zeal for his kingdom drives them to suffer victimally—that is, vicariously—for the sanctification and salvation of others. In union with Jesus crucified and the Mother of Sorrows, these victim-souls offer their sufferings and crosses, their penances and self-denials, for all mankind, particularly those in danger of death and damnation.

Some Outstanding Examples

One immediately thinks in this context of the Fatima seers—that amazing trio of Portuguese children not yet in their teens—who generously prayed and made personal sacrifices at Our Lady's urgent behest. On one occasion, after showing them a glimpse of hell, she exhorted them:

> Pray, pray a good deal, and make sacrifices on behalf of sinners. For many souls go to hell because they have no one to make sacrifices and pray for them.[23]

A multitude of victimal souls vie here for mention; the following happen to be among the better-known examples. First of all, the early St. Ignatius of Loyola, who was very devoted to the Mother of Sorrows, once immersed himself in the frozen Seine to win the grace of conversion for sinners. Then there is the example of St. Bernadette Soubirous and St. Thérèse of Lisieux drawing strength from God's mother to offer, day after day, their hidden sufferings for priests. As for that outstandingly holy priest, the Curé d'Ars, he subjected himself years on end to severe fasting and penance for the sanctification of his parish.

Another victim-soul was Elizabeth Laseur, who was strongly devoted to the queen of the Communion of Saints. From her she won the grace to make a loving oblation of her incurable sickness and death for the conversion of her bitterly atheistic husband. To everyone's amazement, he received that grace soon after her death. And, for good measure, he was given the further grace of a vocation as a Dominican priest—as Elizabeth had foretold.

The mystery of victimal suffering has been much illuminated by Hans Urs von Balthasar's study of St. Elizabeth of the Trinity. It highlights, among other things, the role played by God's mother in guiding and encouraging victim-souls. In St. Elizabeth's own words: "Our Lady is the Queen of Martyrs, the teacher of those who fill up what is wanting in the sufferings of Christ and who suffer with him."[24]

Mary's Priestly Maternity

We have seen that all our human sacrifices and sufferings are subsumed into the Good Friday sacrifice and its mystical renewal on our altars, being drawn there as into a magnetic field of divine grace and love. And through the hands of God's mother our sacrifices and sufferings are presented to that pierced Heart which is in such close alliance with her own.

We have likewise seen how Mary's maternal role is evident in every aspect of Christ's priestly activity, all the way from the cross and the altar to the priesthood of his faithful.

Archbishop Fulton Sheen once described the Redeemer's mother as "the first ciborium of his true presence."[25] He also called her "the sacristan of divine love," because she prepared and presented her Son for his great sacrifice. Furthermore, during his sacrifice, both on the cross and the altar, Emmanuel's mother can in a sense claim with regard to his humanity: "This is my body, and this is my blood."

As will be shown in a subsequent chapter, Mary's maternal role is similarly engaged at a very deep level with the ministerial priesthood, thus bringing her intimately into the lives of those empowered to consecrate the bread and wine and offer the Eucharistic sacrifice. As for the baptismal priesthood, Mary's maternal heart presides over every self-sacrifice and offering made by the faithful both inside and outside of Mass.

Clearly, then, Mary's own priestly status is unique. She did not receive priestly ordination like the apostles; nevertheless, in the order of grace she is far higher than them through being mother of the great High Priest. Mary exercised the priesthood of the faithful—but did so in a pre-eminent and universal way. Her unique priestly status was well summed up by a distinguished theologian:

> Though Mary did not receive the character of priestly Orders, she bore, more than her life-companions, the anointing of the royal priesthood.... She did not have power to consecrate but to offer the pure, full and perfect Host on the altar of her heart, where

the fire of the holocaust burned ceaselessly.[26]

Mary's Unceasing Mission

To sum up, then. Mary's priestly maternity is a profound participation in the priesthood of Christ. And this is because she is dynamically united with his redemptive sacrifice and its Eucharistic renewals. Consequently she is the mother and shining inspiration of all who share at different levels in her Son's priesthood.

Just as the Word Incarnate, true to his promise, remains with us all days—as a Eucharistic Presence, Priest and Victim—even till the end of the world (cf. Mt. 28:20), so does Our Lady of the Blessed Sacrament. For her maternal mission is to lead generation after generation of human souls into the embrace of the Eucharistic Saviour. And she will never cease from this task till He comes again—once his death has for the last time been shown forth in the breaking of bread (cf. 1 Cor. 11:26). As a poet has written:

> The Mother
> Holds him God has forsaken, Word made flesh
> Made ransom, to the slow smoulder of her heart,
> Till the catharsis of the race shall be complete.[27]

---

[1] Arnold of Chartres: DE SEPTEM VERBIS DOMINI, 3 PL 189, 1694
[2] Pope Pius XII: MEDIATOR DEI, 3
[3] Thomas à Kempis: THE IMITATION OF CHRIST, Bk 1V, ch 2
[4] Vatican II: LUMEN GENTIUM, 53
[5] Pope Leo XIII: MIRAE CARITATIS, AAS 34 (1902)
[6] St. Bernard: SERMON 3 ON THE PURIFICATION, PL 183, 3706
[7] Pope St. Pius X: AD DIEM ILLUM, AAS 36 (1903–4)
[8] Vatican II: LUMEN GENTIUM, 58, 61
[9] Pope John Paul II: ANGELUS ADDRESS, 22 February 1983 (Reported in *L'Osserv. Romano*, 2 March 1983)
[10] Pope Pius XII: MEDIATOR DEI, 82
[11] Richard Crashaw: RELIGIOUS POEMS. The Recommendation, (London) 1914
[12] René Laurentin: MARY AND THE EUCHARIST, (Dublin) 1955
[13] St. Peter Julian Eymard: IN THE LIGHT OF THE MONSTRANCE: Edited by Charles DeKeyser, S.S.S., (Cleveland) 1947
[14] Pope John Paul II: ANGELUS ADDRESS, 5 June 1983 (Reported in *L'Osserv. Romano*, 13 June 1983)

---

[15] St. Ignatius Loyola: PERSONAL WRITINGS. Translated with Introduction by Joseph A. Munitiz, S.J. and Philip Endean, S.J. (Penguin Classics) 78, 378

[16] Blessed M. Faustina Kowalska: DIVINE MERCY IN MY SOUL: Diary, (Marian Press) 1987, 87

[17] Padre Pio: A PADRE PIO PROFILE. Letters 1, 312 (St. Bede's Publications) 1987

[18] Alberto D'Apolito: PADRE PIO OF PIETRELCINA: MEMORIES, EXPERIENCES, (San Giovanni Rotondo) 1983

[19] The Marian Movement of Priests: TO THE PRIESTS, OUR LADY'S BELOVED SONS (11th Edit. 1995): Message given on 20 April 1984, 328–329

[20] Vatican II: LUMEN GENTIUM, 65, 61 cf. *Presbyterorum Ordinis*, 5

[21] Vatican II: LUMEN GENTIUM, 34

[22] St. Thomas Aquinas: SUMMA THEOLOGICA, Pars 3, q.82. a.1 (ad In Sent. 1V, d. 13, q.i (ad 1)

[23] John M. Haffert: HER OWN WORDS: THE MEMOIRS OF SR. LUCY (101 Foundation) 1993, 100

[24] Hans Urs von Balthasar: ELIZABETH OF DIJON, (London) 1956, 125

[25] Archbishop Fulton Sheen: PRIVATE LETTER TO THE REVEREND J. L. ANTHAMATTEN, C.P.P.S., 19 September 1949

[26] John Gerson: OPERA OMNIA, IX, 384

[27] David Gascoyne: COLLECTED POEMS: MISERERE, (OUP) 1988

CHAPTER FOUR

Mary and Holy Communion

Leonardo da Vinci is on record as saying that, while working on his immortal Last Supper, his main aim was to portray as closely as possible something of "the infinite sadness of Christ," for whom that poignant farewell meal was so overshadowed by an apostle's treachery.

After his Ascension, Our Lord was to feature in yet another poignant celebration in that same Upper Room. The occasion was the first-ever Eucharistic breaking of bread, at which Mary, along with the disciples, made her first Holy Communion.

To express adequately the depths of her feelings on receiving the body and blood of Jesus would call for the pen of a Shakespeare or Beethoven's musical genius. She who had conceived him who was both her God and her Son welcomed into her heart that same Person now mysteriously present as a consecrated Host. The Mother of Sorrows who had lovingly held in her arms the broken body of the Crucified now embraced his risen Eucharistic Self with an inexpressible combination of maternal love and creaturely worship.

St. Augustine's words come to mind in this context:

> Him whom the heavens cannot contain the womb of one woman bore. She ruled our Ruler. She carried him in whom we all are. She gave milk to our Bread.[1]

That closing phrase ("she gave milk to our Bread") is rich in paradox when we reflect that, during the interval between his

Ascension and Mary's Assumption, the risen Jesus united himself with her chiefly through Holy Communion. Thus the milk of divine grace was now regularly fed to her whose maternal milk had once nourished the living Bread in his infancy. And Mary would therefore have been immeasurably enriched in grace each time she partook of the Lord's body and blood.

Mary and Our Communions

Because Mary is our model in all Eucharistic devotions, not least in the reception of the Blessed Sacrament, St. Maximilian Kolbe gives this advice: "Let Mary prepare us. Let her receive him *with us* in Holy Communion."[2]

This practice has been observed by many of the Lord's closest disciples. For example, St. Thérèse of Lisieux, before every Communion she received, would ask the mother of God to prepare her heart. St. Alphonsus Liguori did likewise. The wisdom of the saints taught him and scores like him that the immaculate Mary, the woman who had given milk to our Bread and who herself received him with inexpressible devotion, is the supreme patroness of all communicants.

Adrienne von Speyr—the mystic closely associated with Hans Urs von Balthasar—wrote very comfortingly about Our Lady's helpful role in our relations with the God of Holy Communion:

> The Virgin Mother was the perfect receiver of her Son, and remains so always and for everyone. Therefore every worthy reception of Communion participates in her perfect reception. She gives something of her innocent and virginal reception of her Son to whoever receives the Host.
>
> Sinful, failing man might recoil at the thought of taking the Lord of all creation into himself. Through the grace of his mother this reception is now robbed of every difficulty; it may now even take place in joy, trust, and an almost soaring light-heartedness.... The communicant no longer needs to struggle at length with his preparation, to wonder if he has done everything in order to approach

> Communion worthily. Through her helping love the mother supplements the Christian at Communion for the reception of her Son.[3]

Mary's Eucharistic Faith and Ours

It was Mary's deep faith that enabled her during the post-Ascension years to maintain the special alliance of hearts between herself and the Eucharistic Jesus. Indeed, as we saw earlier, it was her initial faith in the mystery of the Incarnation and its prolongation in the Eucharist that served not only as model but quasi-matrix of our own faith.

"Blessed art thou, Mary, for thy believing!" (Lk. 1:45). Blessed, too, are we, the believing children begotten through the faith of our believing mother. And nowhere are we more blessed for our believing than when we focus on faith's centrepiece and masterpiece—the Blessed Sacrament.

We clearly owe it to ourselves—let alone to the God of the Eucharist and his mother—to be well-instructed about so sublime a mystery. We owe it equally to faith as such, as the Blessed Virgin has so emphasized at Medjugorje. The reason is that, of its very nature, God's precious gift of faith ever seeks a clearer understanding of the invisible realities it sets before our inward vision. And of these invisible realities none is more deserving of a well-informed faith than this sacramental jewel—the God-Man giving himself to us as Presence, Priest, Victim and Food.

What We Receive in Holy Communion

Belief in the real presence in the consecrated Host—that is, the substantial, corporeal, personal presence of the Son of God—is founded upon the words of institution spoken by him at the Last Supper: "This is my body.... This is my blood" (Lk. 22:15–20).

There is little room for doubt that Our Lord meant his words to be taken literally, not figuratively or metaphorically. Karl Rahner made an illuminating observation on this point:

> What Christ gives us is quite explicit if his own

> words are interpreted according to their Aramaic meaning. The expression "This is my body" means "This is MYSELF." For this reason St. John in his gospel (6:57) has replaced the words "body" and "blood" simply by the phrase: Whoever eats ME.[4]

This has certainly been the traditional belief since Apostolic times. St. Justin in the second century coined the expression "eucharistized bread," making it absolutely clear that the Catholic faith embraces the integral presence of the risen Saviour in the consecrated species. Here are that early witness's exact words:

> Not as common bread or as common drink do we receive these.... We have been taught that the food which has been Eucharistized by the word of prayer, that food which by assimilation nourishes our flesh and blood, is the flesh and blood of the Incarnate Jesus.[5]

The Eucharistic belief of the early Church is absolutely identical with that held by the 16th century poet-martyr:

> The God of hosts in slender Host doth dwell.
> Yea, God and Man with all to either due...
> That God and Man who is the angels' bliss
> In form of bread and wine our nurture is.[6]

The Word Incarnate becomes the Word-made-Eucharist through the formula of consecration spoken by an ordained priest. The effect of this consecration is to Eucharistize—that is, convert, refashion, transmute—the physical reality of bread and wine into that sacred reality which is the glorified God-Man.

Technical and Devotional

The technical term for the conversion of bread and wine into the constitutive being of the Word Incarnate is *transubstantiation*. And this awesome change obviously comes about by a divine intervention in the natural order. The convert Chesterton accepted the mystery of the True Presence with child-like simplicity; he reasoned that, if God could become man, He should have no problem converting himself into the form of bread. Similarly Cardinal Newman experienced no mental blocks or reservations about what transubstantiation entails. He said on this subject:

> It is difficult, impossible to imagine, I grant; but how is it impossible to *believe*? I cannot indeed prove it. I cannot tell *how* it is. But I say, "Why should it not be? What's to hinder it? What do I know of substance or matter? Just as much as the greatest philosophers, and that is nothing at all."[7]

So for us the Blessed Sacrament is no mere symbol of the Lord's presence but his actual bodily Self, whole and entire. Accordingly we adore him there as our Eucharistic Emmanuel and receive him into ourselves as the living bread that comes down from heaven. He offers himself as the Victim of the Mass-sacrifice, one purpose of which is to make himself available as our spiritual food. And, as St. John Vianney used to say, the food remaining over from the sacrificial banquet is reserved in the tabernacle as in a sacred pantry or larder.

Would that we could all have the vivid Mary-like faith and devotion that breathes through the beautiful old Irish prayer. During the dark days of persecution it was said by the faithful on receiving Communion: "Welcome, a thousand welcomes, white love of my heart, welcome within me!"

The Fruits of Communion

A striking feature of all Marian shrines is that they are profoundly Eucharistic. In her respective messages, the Blessed Virgin warmly encourages pilgrims to receive Communion frequently, because none knows better than she the rich spiritual benefits that flow from this source.

First and foremost of these benefits is that Communion preserves, augments and revitalizes the life of grace given to us at Baptism. Now "life of grace" is really a synonym for union with

Christ. And it is towards an ever-closer union of the faithful with himself, the living bread, that our High Priest directs his sacrifice in the first place.

The altar itself represents the Eucharist's dual aspect as sacrifice and sacrament. For that is where Christ offers his life *for* us as Victim; and, on the other hand, the altar is the table of the Lord where He offers himself *to* us as Communion. In both capacities the altar serves to build up the union between our souls and the Eucharistic Saviour.

This all-important union is enshrined in the gospel text: "He who eats my flesh and drinks my blood abides in me and I in him.... As the living Father sent me and I live by the Father, so he who eats me will live because of me" (Jn. 6:56–57).

Early Christian writers dwelt long on the amazing truth that in his great love for us the God of heaven and earth actually becomes our sacramental guest and food. St. Cyril of Alexandria, for example, wrote:

> When we ingest the Eucharist, in reality we are ingesting the Godhead. This makes of us a kind of tabernacle, and we are transformed. For thus we become Christ-bearers, because his body and blood are diffused through our members ... and we become partakers of the divine nature.[8]

What this amounts to saying is that, even though we physically assimilate the sacramental Christ as nourishment, it is really He who assimilates us. And this, Archbishop Fulton Sheen points out, is fully in keeping with the so-called law of transformation. Just as chemicals are transformed by assimilation into plants, plants into animals, and animals into man, so man is transformed into God—but without losing his personal identity. Therefore, Sheen concludes, "it is not so much we who receive Christ as Christ who receives us, incorporating us into Himself."[9]

Conversion and Charity

Holy Communion is also closely connected with our Christian

commitment to continual conversion and the pursuit of holiness. This theme is like a recurring refrain in Our Lady's instructions given at Fatima, Medjugorje and other shrines. In fact, she is simply echoing the biblical injunction: "He that is holy, let him be holier still" (Apoc. 22:11).

Another effect of Holy Communion is purification of conscience. As the *Catholic Catechism* makes clear, "the Eucharist cannot unite us to Christ without cleansing us from past sins and preserving us from future ones."[10]

The charity kindled in us by the Eucharistic Heart of Jesus wipes away venial sins and helps us to break away from any disordered attachment to creatures. Similarly the sacrament fortifies us against future mortal sins and the temptations of evil spirits. St. John Chrysostom thus exhorts those who have received Christ's Body at the altar: "Let us go forth from that table like lions breathing out fire, terrible in the sight of devils."[11]

But of a different kind are the effects of Eucharistic fire on our human relations generally. The saint who first applied to Mary the title Mother of the Blessed Sacrament said of Holy Communion:

> It is a fire whose heat will warm and cheer those around you. They will breathe the Eucharistic presence. The sweetness which you will draw from your Communion will have its effect on your conduct, and will soon attract all hearts, first to yourself, and then to him whom you carry in your breast. Have faith in the influence of the presence of the Lord.[12]

The Eucharist is essentially Viaticum—that is, journey-food for our long pilgrimage through this world to the City of God beyond. Our pilgrim-way, as we all experience over the years, is liable to be beset with crosses, problems and difficulties. We need strength and solace as we strive daily to keep going, to triumph over trials and temptations, and, above all, to make steady progress in our love and service of God and neighbour. St. Francis of Sales offers this golden advice:

> Your principal motive in going to Communion should be to advance, strengthen and console yourself in the love of God, receiving for love alone what is given for love alone.... If you are asked why you go to Communion so often, say it is to learn to love God, to be purified from your imperfections, delivered from your miseries, consoled in your troubles, and strengthened in your weaknesses.... By adoring and feeding on beauty, purity and goodness itself in the Eucharist, you will become altogether beautiful, pure and good.[13]

In its liturgy the Church repeatedly reminds us of the Eucharist's supportive role amidst life's tensions and trials. The post-Communion prayer for the feast of the Holy Family goes to the heart of the matter:

> Eternal Father, we want to live as Jesus, Mary and Joseph did in peace with you and one another. May this Communion strengthen us to face the trials of life.

Unity of Christ's Body

The mother of the Church, while preparing us to receive Holy Communion with maximum spiritual profit, also helps us to keep the sacrament's wider social outreach in focus. For Christ our Head, through uniting us personally to himself in the Host, unites us at the same time all the more closely with fellow-members of his Mystical Body—that is, the faithful who comprise the Church.

When speaking of the Mystical Body, we must always bear in mind that the mother of its Head loves each and every individual member as a precious son or daughter. In St. Lawrence of Brindisi's words, "Mary cherishes us with maternal charity, with intimate, true, heartfelt love."[14] So for her the term "Mystical Body" is no mere abstraction; rather, it stands for her very own and beloved spiritual family, the universal community of the Lord's brothers and sisters, for each of whom her Immaculate Heart beats with the tender love of a mother.

Mary has this universal family in mind when she encourages us—indeed, urges us—as she did at Fatima to make reparation on its behalf by offering, among other things, our Holy Communion on five consecutive First Saturdays of the month.

Our personal incorporation into this worldwide family commences at Baptism; in which sacrament, St. Paul teaches, we have been called to form one Body (cf. 1 Cor. 12:13). And our baptismal incorporation into this worldwide Body is renewed, strengthened and deepened by every Holy Communion we receive. "Because there is one bread," runs the familiar Pauline formula, "we who are many are one Body, for we all partake of the one bread" (1 Cor. 10:16–17).

Communion with the Church

What the foregoing text equivalently tells us is that the Eucharist, besides symbolizing the Church's unity, is the very instrument and agency that produces unity in the first place and serves to sustain it. To quote an official Church document:

> The Eucharist is the efficacious sign and sublime cause of that communion in the divine life and that unity of the People of God by which the Church is kept in being.[15]

To be in full communion with the Church is therefore required of all approaching sacramental Communion. The Holy See has nonetheless encouraged a degree of intercommunion with the separated Eastern Churches, because they are "still joined to us in the closest intimacy" through possessing true sacraments, notably Holy Orders and the Eucharist.[16]

Different, however, is the situation with regard to those Protestant ecclesial communities which, as a result of their initial separation from the Church, lack the sacrament of Holy Orders and consequently the fullness of the Eucharistic reality.[17] For this reason, the same degree of intercommunion as the foregoing cannot be applied.

But in cases of serious necessity the local Ordinary may

permit any Christians of whatever denomination to receive Holy Communion (as well as the sacraments of Penance and Anointing) if they ask for them, and provided they believe what Catholics do as regards the sacrament in question. Further, for the reception of Holy Communion they must satisfy the required dispositions as to fasting, etc.

Receiving Holy Communion Worthily

Our Lord has exhorted us to receive him in the sacrament of his love, for "unless we eat his flesh and drink his blood we will not have life in ourselves" (Jn. 6:53). An indication of his eager desire to make us the gift of Holy Communion is seen in his words at the Last Supper: "I have longed and longed to share this paschal meal with you before my passion" (Lk. 22:15).

Numerous Christian writers have dwelt upon the consuming love that prompts the Second Person of the Trinity to offer himself for us and to us in the sacrament of the altar. St. Gregory of Nazianzen says that God thirsts for the return-thirst of our love. And St. Thomas Aquinas describes the Eucharistic Christ as a divine hunger in search of our return-hunger for him.

Clearly, then, we must respond generously to such tremendous love—and duly prepare to receive this august, all-holy Guest under the roof of our selfhood, our shabby, sinful, unworthy selfhood. St. Bonaventure likened those receiving Communion to the devout Simeon receiving the infant Jesus into his arms from his gracious young mother.[18] How ardent therefore must be her desire that the fruit of her womb be received into hearts full of faith and free from sin.

Indeed, in preparing for Holy Communion our foremost duty is to examine our conscience and, if need be, purify it, through the sacrament of Reconciliation, of any hitherto unconfessed grave sin(s). The Church in her *Code of Canon Law* strictly enjoins this on the faithful (Canon 916). And hereby she echoes St. Paul's insistence on a good conscience as being an indispensable condition for receiving Communion worthily:

> And therefore, if anyone eats this bread or drinks

> this cup of the Lord unworthily, he will be held to account for the Lord's body and blood. A man must examine himself first, and then eat of that bread and drink of that cup; he is eating and drinking damnation to himself if he eats and drinks unworthily, not recognizing the Lord's body for what it is (1 Cor. 11:27–29).

Divorced and Remarried

A certain amount of controversy has recently arisen about the situation of divorced Catholics who have entered invalidly into a second marriage. The question is: do they legitimately—that is, worthily—receive Holy Communion? The Vatican issued an official ruling on this subject, basing its negative response on the vital bond between the Eucharistic Christ and his Mystical Body. The text runs:

> If the divorced are remarried civilly, they find a situation that objectively contradicts God's law. Consequently they cannot receive Holy Communion as long as this situation persists.
>
> This norm is not at all a punishment or a discrimination against the divorced and remarried, but rather expresses an objective situation that of itself renders impossible the reception of Holy Communion. They are unable to be admitted thereto from the fact that their state and condition of life objectively contradicts that union of love between Christ and his Church, which is signified and effected by the Eucharist. Besides this ... if these people were admitted to the Eucharist, the faithful would be led into error and confusion regarding the Church's teaching about the indissolubility of marriage.[19]

Sacrilegious Communions

Karl Rahner speaks for many bishops and priests when he asks the following question:

> Are average Catholics today sufficiently aware of the obligation of going to Confession before receiving Communion when they have committed a serious sin?[20]

Pope John Paul II has on several occasions expressed serious concern over the high incidence of sacrilegious Communions. And this worrying state of affairs is amply corroborated by the testimony of many priests engaged in pastoral ministry. They report that it is by no means uncommon to encounter penitents who have serious guilt to confess—yet who admit that they have nonetheless been receiving Holy Communion in the meantime.

One recalls that at Pellevoisin—and subsequently at Garabandal, Medjugorje and other shrines—Our Lady referred to the grave guilt attaching to sacrilegious Communions. And she often dwells sorrowfully on this theme in her messages through Fr. Stefano Gobbi. For instance:

> It is sacrileges that today form around my Immaculate Heart a painful crown of thorns. At this present time how many Communions are made—and how many sacrileges perpetrated! It can be said that there is no longer any Eucharistic celebration where sacrilegious Communions are not made. If you only saw with my eyes how great is this wound that has contaminated the whole Church, paralyzing it, halting it, and making it impure and so very sick. If you only saw with my eyes, you would shed copious tears with me.[21]

A major cause of this grave situation is, as Rahner indicates, the serious decline in the practice of Confession. To make matters worse, many of the younger generation nowadays have received inadequate instruction as to the meaning of sin and the role of the confessional. Often enough, too, those receiving Communion sacrilegiously are quite unaware of the strict obligation to confess serious guilt beforehand.

Role of the Confessional

Clearly the remedy for this disturbing state of affairs is to restore the confessional to its former place of honour in catechetics and pastoral life alike. This would help to restore the practice of frequent Confession—a practice which has been warmly recommended by a whole string of recent popes.

Not surprisingly, then, frequent Confession is strongly urged by Our Lady at Medjugorje; she insists that every single one of us should confess our sins *at least once a month*. And she assures us, for good measure, that, if this practice were universally adopted, the Church's current malaise would soon be healed.

This chimes in with what St. Thomas teaches about the sacrament of Confession; its fundamental role, he says, is to prepare us for a more worthy reception of that greatest of all sacraments: the Lord's body in the Eucharist.[22] For the saint saw full well that in the Blessed Sacrament is contained, as the Vatican Council was later to declare, "the Church's entire spiritual wealth."[23]

Another factor accounting for the high incidence of bad Communions is the widespread erosion of belief in the Lord's true presence in the sacrament. Instead it is widely regarded as a mere symbol or reminder of Christ's Presence.

Furthermore, many younger Catholics today have been brought up to believe that the Mass is not so much a sacrifice as simply a commemorative meal, a fellowship celebration, at which all present, including people of other religions or none, are invited to partake of the ritual bread and wine—the elements that in a purely symbolic and spiritual way evoke the spiritual presence of Jesus and re-create the atmosphere of the Last Supper.

Spiritual Union

"He has filled the hungry with good things" (Lk. 1:53). Mary's song of gratitude applies very closely to us privileged to receive what is the very best of all "good things"—the sacred body born of her and now made food for our souls. More than that, this food remains permanently with us as an abiding presence in our tabernacles. For this we owe him our heartfelt thanksgiving and adoration—as the following chapter sets out.

---

[1] St. Augustine: SERMON 184, 2, 3, PL 38, 997

[2] St. Maximilian Kolbe: WRITINGS OF MAXIMILIAN KOLBE: A FOCOLARE COLLECTION, 1988, 475

[3] Adrienne von Speyr: HANDMAID OF THE LORD. (San Francisco) 1985, 153–154

[4] Karl Rahner, S.J.: ON VISITING THE BLESSED SACRAMENT, Geist und Leben, 1959

[5] St. Justin Martyr: APOLOGIA, 1, 62

[6] St. Robert Southwell: POEMS AND PROSE WRITINGS: OF THE BLESSED SACRAMENT OF THE ALTAR (London) 1937

[7] John Henry Cardinal Newman: APOLOGIA PRO VITA SUA. (Oxford) 1967, ch. 5

[8] St. Cyril of Alexandria: CATECHETICAL LECTURES, 4, 6

[9] Archbishop Fulton Sheen: THIS IS THE MASS. (New York) 164

[10] CATECHISM OF THE CATHOLIC CHURCH. (Veritas) 1994, # 1393

[11] St. John Chrysostom: IN JOANN. HOM. 61, 3, PG 59, 260

[12] St. Peter Julian Eymard: IN THE LIGHT OF THE MONSTRANCE: Edited by Charles DeKeyser, S.S.S., (Cleveland) 1947

[13] St. Francis of Sales: AN INTRODUCTION TO THE DEVOUT LIFE, (London) 1943, 91–92

[14] St. Lawrence of Brindisi: MARIALE, (Padua) 1964, n. 83

[15] Sacred Congregation of Rites: UNITATIS REDINTEGRATIO, 15, #2 cf. *Code of Canon Law*, can. 844, #3

[16] op. cit. 22, 3. cff. CODE OF CANON LAW, can.844, #4; *Catechism of Catholic Church*, #1399

[17] CATECHISM OF THE CATHOLIC CHURCH. (Veritas) 1994, #1400

[18] St. Bonaventure: SERMON 3 DE CORPORE CHRISTI, Opera Omnia 5, 559b

[19] Sacred Congregation for the Doctrine of Faith: LETTER TO THE WORLD'S BISHOPS, 14 October 1994

[20] Karl Rahner, S.J.: EUCHARISTIC DEVOTION: THEOLOGICAL INVESTIGATIONS, 23, (London) 1992, 114

[21] The Marian Movement of Priests: TO THE PRIESTS, OUR LADY'S BELOVED SONS (11th Edit. 1995): Message given on 8 August 1986, 390

[22] St. Thomas Aquinas: SUMMA THEOLOGICA, Pars 3, q.7, a.3

[23] Vatican II: PREBYTERORUM ORDINIS, 5

CHAPTER FIVE

Mary and Eucharistic Adoration

"Teach us, O Mary, the life of adoration."[1] St. Peter Eymard's prayer highlights the fact that the mother of the Eucharist is its primary adorer. And her adoration is literally perpetual, in keeping with the "indissoluble bond" uniting her now and forever with the Word Incarnate. Mary is therefore ideally suited to instruct us in the ways of Eucharistic adoration.

So closely is Mary united with the Godhead, so profound is her worship, and so ardent and adoring, in every sense, is her mother-love for the Eucharistic Jesus, that she out-adores and out-loves even the highest angelic spirits. At the same time, Mary's mother-love for her pilgrim children on earth fills her with the desire to guide our steps towards the tabernacle.

Certainly this was the case with St. Peter Eymard. He always maintained it was Mary who led him in the first place to the practice of Eucharistic adoration, and then to make its promotion his full-time apostolate.

Eucharist Among Lepers

Our Lady has led many another chosen soul to a life of intimacy with the Eucharistic Lord. One notable example was the heroic Fr. Damien; known as the "apostle of the lepers," he was beatified in 1995. As a young priest he volunteered to work in Hawaii on the island of Molokai, to which lepers were ostracized from both family and society because the disease was so contagious and, in those mid-nineteenth-century days, still incurable.

Fr. Damien spent the rest of his life among these wretched outcasts with their rotting flesh and hideously mutilated faces and limbs. And, to crown it all, he himself inevitably contracted the dread disease and died of it.

His devotion to the mother of God had drawn him almost magnetically towards the Eucharist. And this proved to be his rock and his mainstay on Molokai. To a friend asking how he could possibly keep going in such humanly unbearable conditions, he confessed: "Without my daily holy hour before the Blessed Sacrament I could not have stood it for one single day."

Adoration by Lepers

Moreover, this great devotee of Eucharistic adoration did all he could to share that treasure with his pathetic charges. Having first built a little chapel, he catechized them carefully as to the meaning of Mass, the real presence and Holy Communion. Next he set up perpetual adoration of the Blessed Sacrament, to which they took with intense faith and ardour. Fr. Damien testified that some most touching and memorable prayers came spontaneously to the lips of those outcast adorers.

One particular leper's prayer was unmatched for its originality and child-like directness and charm. During his daily Holy Hour he would spend his time praising and thanking the great Creator, now before him in sacramental form, for the many beautiful things He gives us in this world. And he would go on to enumerate some of them, including "the sound of the waves, the cry of the sea-birds, the blue of the ocean, the wheat and the flowers that spring from the ground, the sunsets that splash the western sky with gorgeous colours."

Come, Let Us Adore Him

Presently we shall turn our attention to the practical and devotional aspects of this jewel among Catholic devotions. But first let us consider how perfectly the cult of the Eucharist fulfils our basic creaturely duty—and need—to adore our Creator and Redeemer.

"Man was created to praise, reverence and serve God our Lord." St. Ignatius' celebrated formula expresses the bottom line itself of man's meaning and destiny. Similarly the first commandment clearly spells out God's rights over us and our corresponding duties towards him. As for Scripture, it is saturated with these selfsame truths, enjoining us in text after text to offer our sovereign Lord the cult of latria—that is, worship, adoration, praise.

Now one of the many benefits of Eucharistic adoration is that it provides a convenient and intimate way of paying the divine Being the worship that is his due. Fr. Frederick Faber summed this up most concisely. "The Blessed Sacrament," he said, "is God. So devotion to the Blessed Sacrament is simply divine worship."[2]

This highly-rewarding practice has been part of our Catholic heritage from earliest times, as the Church reaffirmed against the sixteenth-century-Protestant reformers, most of whom denied Christ's true presence in the consecrated Host, let alone the possibility of adoring him there.[3]

Hence with full justification we can direct towards the Eucharistic presence such texts as "Let all the angels of God adore him" (Heb. 1:6; Ps. 96:7), as well as gospel episodes referring to the adoration given to Christ at Bethlehem by the Magi (Mt. 2:11) as also by the apostles at the Ascension (Mt. 28:17).

Adoration Under Attack

Another preliminary needs to be addressed before we proceed to examine the main features and forms of this treasured devotion.

Not a few theologians and liturgists with pronounced liberal leanings are opposed to the cult of adoration paid to consecrated Hosts reserved in the tabernacle. What, then, we may ask, are their objections to Eucharistic adoration?

One is the contention that the sacrament's authentic values lie exclusively in the liturgy—that is, Mass and Holy Communion. As for the adoration of Hosts outside Mass, this they reject as being static, unliturgical, conducive to a narrowly self-centred, pietistic and even anti-communitarian spirituality. These critics further stigmatize adoration as an extra-liturgical exaggeration that crept in a good while after the Church's foundation.

Pope Paul VI vigorously countered these errors, pointing out that the Church has always encouraged the cult of this sacrament both inside and outside of Mass by carefully reserving consecrated Hosts and exposing them to solemn veneration; also by carrying them on special occasions, to the joy of the faithful, in public processions.[4]

Pope John Paul II in turn has proved to be a tireless defender and apostle of Eucharistic adoration. To give this example:

> Public and private devotion to the Eucharist outside Mass is highly recommended. For the presence of Christ, who is adored by the faithful in the sacrament, derives from the sacrifice and is directed towards sacramental and spiritual Communion.[5]

Adoration's Worldwide Links

The truth is that Eucharistic adoration is anything but narrowly self-centred and pietistic; rather, it links us up in a great adventure of faith and love with the vast Communion of Saints, thereby elevating our prayer into an instrument of grace for our brothers and sisters the world over. Thus the entire Church receives an enrichment from our silent vigils before the sacrament of love. To quote the Holy Father once more:

> Closeness to the Eucharistic Christ in silence and contemplation does not distance us from our contemporaries but, on the contrary, makes us open to human joy and distress, broadening our hearts on a global scale. Through adoration the Christian mysteriously contributes to the radical transformation of the world and to the sowing of the gospel. Anyone who prays to the Eucharistic Saviour draws the whole world with him and raises it to God.[6]

But the dissenters in question tend to remain strongly opposed to devotions such as visits before the tabernacle, benediction of the Blessed Sacrament, solemn Eucharistic processions, adoration of the Blessed Sacrament exposed, and perpetual adoration in parish churches.

Cardinal Ratzinger has vigorously rebutted all objections to these time-honoured manifestations of Eucharistic devotion. For example, in defence of Corpus Christi processions, which are held in particular scorn by dissident theologians and liturgists, he writes:

> The Corpus Christi processions so loved by the people should be retained. Here again the liturgical "archeologists" voice their objections and point out that these processions did not exist in the Roman Church during the first centuries. But we must recognize that the instinct of faith possessed by the Catholic people is able, as the centuries proceed, to draw forth all the consequences of the inheritance entrusted to them, to plumb that inheritance and bring it into the light of day.[7]

Prescence—and Presences

The Sovereign Pontiff, preaching during exposition of the Blessed Sacrament during the Eucharistic Congress in Seville, began by saying:

> United with the angels and saints of the heavenly Church, let us adore the most holy sacrament of the Eucharist.[8]

These words were far from being mere rhetoric. Rather, they affirm the reality that all God's angels and saints, in unison with their queen and ours, co-adore the Eucharist along with ourselves. Indeed, they are quite literally *perpetual adorers*. Furthermore, these co-adoring presences are always pleased to encourage and support our own humble efforts.

Few can have made more extensive use of the ever-ready help available from our heavenly friends than did St. Alphonsus Liguori, who cherished the Blessed Sacrament as his "paradise on earth."[9] One of his favourite ejaculations was: "Mary, my mother, my patron saints and angels in heaven, help me to love my God."

What we come to realize very clearly from the foregoing is that our Eucharistic Emmanuel is far from being "all on his own" in the tabernacle. On the contrary, the entire court of heaven, including its gracious queen, is perpetually and adoringly at his side. So, within what may be called the ambiance of the tabernacle, the eyes of faith learn to discern, besides and beside the divine presence, his loving mother plus an innumerable throng of adoring angelic and human spirits.

The Panorama of Faith

Awareness of these millionfold attendant presences brings home to us the grandeur and limitless perspectives of the Eucharistic mystery. And, whereas we but see, through the mists and shadows of faith, the Second Person of the Trinity in his lowly sacramental guise, his mother and the heavenly court behold, without ceasing, in that face-to-face experience we call the beatific vision, his humanity bathed in the radiance and splendour of the Godhead.

This vast assembly of heavenly co-adorers is located, so to speak, within what may variously be described as the ambiance, the surrounds, the zone, the domain, the milieu, the area, of the tabernacled presence. Now as we know all too well, our human perception of anyone's presence necessarily involves categories of a spatial kind, since our imagination is inseparably wedded to the material world. For this reason the bread of life, in making actual his presence among us, accommodates himself to our human psychology to the extent of using the outward appearances—including spatiality—of material elements.

As for Christ's mother, his angels and his saints, they live, like himself, in the celestial world, which transcends space and time. However, their presence alongside the Eucharist conforms to their non-spatial mode of existence in heaven—that transcendent world which is now their eternal habitat.

Two All-Important Presences

Let us also note that there are two further—and profoundly august—presences in the vicinity of the tabernacle. We refer, of course, to God the Father and God the Holy Spirit. Because these two divine Persons are bonded, substantially, intimately, inseparably, into the selfsame being and Godhead as the Second Person present in the Eucharist, they, too, are perpetually with him.

It follows, therefore, that the Eternal Father and the Holy Spirit also and necessarily feature within the amazing panorama spread out before the eyes of faith when contemplating the Eucharistic mystery. What follows no less necessarily is that the Father and the Holy Spirit equally receive the adoration that we on earth—plus Mary and all our co-adorers in heaven—pay to the God-Man in the tabernacle.

In the following chapter we shall be examining the Trinitarian dimension of the Eucharist more closely.

The Mother of Adorers

St. Peter Eymard hailed Our Lady as "the mother of all adorers of the Blessed Sacrament."[10] She has several times endorsed this title in her messages to Fr. Stefano Gobbi, also confirming that she, united with the entire Church in heaven and in purgatory as well, perpetually adores the Trinity in that sacred area centred upon the tabernacle. One of these messages reads:

> Your heavenly mother, with her glorified body that permits her to be both here and in every other place, is truly near every tabernacle in which Jesus is kept. My Immaculate Heart becomes for him a living, beating, motherly tabernacle of love, of adoration, of thanksgiving, and of perpetual adoration.
>
> At your bidding, Jesus becomes present in the Eucharist and is placed in the safekeeping of the tabernacle, surrounded by my motherly heart. Close to the Son there is always the real presence of the Father and the real presence of the Holy Spirit....

> But, as in heaven, so also at the side of every tabernacle, there is the enraptured and joyful presence of your heavenly mother. Then there are all the angels, arranged in their nine choirs of light, to sing ... the omnipotence of the most Holy Trinity.... About the choirs of angels are all the saints and the blessed.... To this summit of paradise there also ascend the profound aspirations, the purifying sufferings and unceasing prayers, of all the souls in purgatory....
>
> This is why, there at the side of Jesus, I am the joyful mother of the Eucharist.[11]

The Adoring Angels and Saints

In the Preface of every Mass we link our adoration with that of the angels when we address our triple "holy" to "the God of power and might." This is further evidence of the Church's belief that the angelic spirits unbrokenly adore the Godhead truly present in our midst. And a whole array of Scriptural texts testify likewise.

St. Margaret Mary informs us in her Autobiography that it was once during adoration of the Blessed Sacrament that angels appeared in order to verify that they were ever united with her in offering God "a continual homage of adoration, praise and love."

Blessed Faustina Kowalska had a similar experience while adoring the Eucharistic Jesus; she recorded it in the form of a prayer:

> O King of glory, though you hide your beauty, yet the eye of my soul rends the veil. I see the angelic choirs giving you honour without cease.[12]

Again, it was through Our Lady's intervention that Catherine Labouré in Paris and Sr. Agnes of Akita were initially conducted to the tabernacle by their angel guardians. Among the lessons we may infer from this is that, after our heavenly mother, no one is keener to guide our steps towards Eucharistic adoration— and to co-adore along with us—than that particular angel God has given each of us as a lifelong guardian, companion and counsellor.

The Master Is Present

"The Master is present and bids us come" (Jn. 11:28). This message delivered by Martha to her sister was echoed by St. John Vianney in his own inimitable way; pointing to the tabernacle he would appeal in these words to his congregation: "He who loves us so much is there, waiting for us. Why do we not love him in return?"

We have already noted a common feature of all Marian apparitions: the mother of the Blessed Sacrament invites us, incessantly and warmly, to maintain a close union of adoration and reparation with our divine guest. Her poignant farewell words to a Garabandal visionary were really addressed to us all: "Conchita," she said, "why don't you visit my Son in the tabernacle more often? He awaits you there all day and all night."[13]

Furthermore, a whole succession of recent popes have constantly exhorted the faithful to visit the Blessed Sacrament on a regular basis. And they themselves certainly practised what they preached. St. Pius X, the so-called "Eucharistic Pope," spent every available moment adoring his Eucharistic Master.

Much the same could be said of all his successors. John XXIII relates how the Lord's mother inspired him early on in life to spend as much time as possible with her Eucharistic Son. Thus he could later record: "My life seems destined to be spent in the light irradiating from the tabernacle."[14]

As for John Paul I, when asked why he habitually wore that radiant smile of his, replied with child-like simplicity: "Because Jesus in the Blessed Sacrament loves me so much." His successor has described visits to the Blessed Sacrament (he himself makes them repeatedly every day) as "a great treasure of our Catholic faith."[15]

Some Saintly Adorers

When we turn to the saints and mystics, we find ourselves in the company of spiritual giants—invariably giants of Eucharistic devotion linked with an intimate love of Mary. Their secret is that they know the rewards of being in that privileged place—that Tabor which is the tabernacle—where the transfigured Jesus in his Eucharistic guise can be addressed in Peter's words: "Lord, it is good for us to be here" (Mk. 9:4).

To help our own modest efforts in the matter, let us look at some random examples of Eucharistic adoration among God's holy ones. All without exception acknowledged that they acquired this devotion, and grew to love it more and more, in what is often called "the school of Mary."

To begin with St. Francis of Assisi. He spent literally his every spare moment adoring the Blessed Sacrament; and, largely moved by his example, so did St. Clare. Saints Dominic and Ignatius, their heavy workload notwithstanding, made frequent visits to the chapel—and exhorted their spiritual sons to do likewise. The same applied to St. Alphonsus Liguori; one of his favourite Eucharistic invocations is a gem of its kind:

> O God-Man present in this sacrament for me—what a comfort, what a privilege to know I kneel before God! And to think that this God loves me!... Mary, my mother, help me to love him in return.[16]

St. John Bosco, through being an ardent client of Our Lady Help of Christians, became an equally ardent devotee of the Blessed Sacrament, encouraging his young charges to visit their "best Friend" as often as possible. As for the life of Charles de Foucauld, it became totally centred on the mystery of Emmanuel abiding among us as Eucharistic bread.

Then there was that amazing prodigy of divine grace—the little nine-year-old Francisco Marto, one of the Fatima visionaries. By following his heavenly mother's instructions, he became inseparably attached to "the hidden God," as he called the divine Person in the tabernacle.

Another spiritual giant who owed his zeal for Eucharistic adoration to his love for Mary was St. Maximilian Kolbe; his colleagues testified that through his tremendous devotion to "the

Immaculate One" he was drawn magnet-like to her Eucharistic Son.

Some More Saintly Adorers

Now for some parallel examples of women saints outstanding for their devotion to our sacramental Saviour. St. Catherine of Siena spent literally every spare moment in his presence. As for St. Teresa of Ávila, through being closely devoted to Mary she developed an irresistible attraction towards the mystery of Jesus in his sacrament of love. Much the same applied to her fellow-Carmelite namesake in Lisieux.

Significantly, it was during exposition of the Blessed Sacrament that the Lord revealed his Sacred Heart to St. Margaret Mary. As for that great modern apostle of the Sacred Heart—St. Frances Xavier Cabrini—the Christ of the tabernacle and his mother ever adoring at his side became the guiding beacons of her life and apostolate.

Decline of Eucharistic Piety

We can never be thankful enough to God for giving us such starlight examples of holiness and piety towards this the greatest of his sacraments. Today's Church stands in sore need of the light and warmth God's heroes and heroines shed through their example. For, alas, Eucharistic piety, not least the custom of paying visits to the Blessed Sacrament, has declined to a worrying degree. Karl Rahner voiced the concern of many when he wrote:

> When we honestly consider the present life of the Church, we cannot deny that Eucharistic piety has experienced a certain decline. Is adoration before the tabernacle still practised as it used to be in the past?... Genuflecting before the Blessed Sacrament is frequently omitted.... This worshipping of Jesus in the sacrament must not be dropped.
>
> It should not be unusual for believers to kneel at times in private prayer before the Lord who saved us. They pray silently; they allow the quiet peace of the

> sacrament to fill them; they tell this sacramentally present Lord about their concerns. But ultimately they only desire to be introduced by Jesus into the truth and love of God which radiate silently from the sacramental sign.
>
> It seems to me that today, and in the future, we must not forget what our Christian forebears practised. The sanctuary lamp of our Catholic churches continues to invite us to a silent lingering before the mystery of our redemption.[17]

Tips for Eucharistic Adoration

This devotion fits easily into prayer's four basic forms— adoration, thanksgiving, reparation, and petition. In actual practice, many of us find that our prayer before the tabernacle commonly tends to veer between all four forms, depending on our particular circumstances and needs at the time.

Greatly to be recommended on all occasions is a preparatory prayer to the Holy Spirit for guidance in how to spend each precious minute before the Blessed Sacrament. Its leading adorer —Mary, Queen of the Angels—is always ready to assist our feeble efforts to co-adore with her and all the blessed spirits, including our own special guardian.

St. Ignatius counsels us to recollect ourselves immediately prior to entering the chapel; thus we are primed to focus our minds straightaway on the Holy of Holies without undue delay or distraction.

More Tips for Eucharistic Adoration

One particularly helpful guideline during adoration is: never feel worried if you find you have no thoughts at all, let alone feelings of devotion. The all-important factor is that you yourself are here and now before the Lord, a personal presence before the Divine Presence of him who knows you inside-out, who can read your innermost thoughts, and who loves you immensely.

"He just looks at me, and I look at him"—thus did one of St. John Vianney's parishioners describe how he spent his time in chapel. And the saintly pastor warmly approved this practice and recommended it to others. He once compared adoration to spiritual sunbathing; just by being in that all-holy presence, he reasoned, you expose yourself to the warmth, the grace and the love radiating from the sacred Host.

Much the same advice was given by Fr. William Doyle:

> If you feel drawn to rest in God, to let yourself sink down, as it were, into him, do so without bothering to say anything. I think the best of all prayers is just to kneel (or sit) quietly and let Jesus pour himself into your soul.[18]

We are given similar counsel from another outstanding apostle of the Blessed Sacrament in our time—Sr. Briege McKenna. She relates how on one occasion during adoration she told the Eucharistic Jesus that she couldn't think of anything to say except tell him that she loved him. The sequel was:

> I felt as though the Lord said to me, "Well, don't you know that you haven't got to say anything to me? Just be with me. Come into my presence. It's not what you do for me. It's what I want to do for you."[19]

It is a good general rule to follow our spiritual attractions in choosing how to pass the time during adoration. Some people read Scripture or spiritual books. Others confine themselves to ejaculatory prayer, even repeating the same ejaculation over and over again. St. Francis of Assisi would spend long hours just repeating the formula: "My Lord and my God."

The Rosary and Adoration

One common and highly recommended practice is to say the Rosary. Let us note that a plenary indulgence may be gained, under the usual conditions, if one recites five decades in a church or chapel where the sacrament is reserved.

"Hail Mary, full of grace, the Lord is with thee." The familiar words take on a dynamic literalness in the context of adoration, since the sacramental Lord and his adoring mother are both actually there—and very near to each other in every sense. Many saints habitually recited the Rosary during adoration. So has a succession of recent popes, one of whom—John XXIII—made a moving reference in his personal diary to this practice:

> My day must be one long prayer: prayer is the breath of my life. I propose to recite all fifteen decades of the Rosary every day, if possible in the chapel before the Blessed Sacrament.... Lord, may I have the grace to do two things well: my visit, and the Rosary. All the rest will follow.
>
> O Jesus in the Blessed Sacrament, I would like to be filled with love for you.... O Mary of the Rosary, keep me recollected when I say these prayers of yours; bind me forever with your Rosary to Jesus of the Blessed Sacrament. Blessed be Jesus, my love; blessed be the Immaculate Virgin Mary.[20]

The Time Factor

The Curé d'Ars related an amusing story about a friend of his, a certain Monsieur de Vidaud, who (doubtless inspired by the holy priest's own example) spent long hours daily before the tabernacle. Indeed, he would rise very early to begin as soon as the church was opened.

One morning they had to send someone three times from his chateau to call him for breakfast, because the mistress of the house was understandably growing impatient. At the third summons (it was now about nine o'clock) the good man finally tore himself away from his devotions with the plaintive remark: "Lord, one is not even permitted nowadays to spend a few quiet moments in peace with you." He had been there since four that morning!

A common and highly commendable practice in Eucharistic adoration is the Holy Hour. It derives directly from the Sacred Heart revelations made to St. Margaret Mary; one of the Saviour's requests was that she should spread the practice of weekly Holy Hour in expiation for the sins of the world. He further requested that, if possible, it should be made on Thursday evenings between 11 and midnight. This practice was clearly linked with the Saviour's Agony in the Garden and his words: "Could you not watch one hour with me?" (Mt. 26:40).

The Holy Hour adoration is practised by many people on a daily, not just weekly, basis. Pope John Paul II, like several of his predecessors, particularly urges priests to take up the practice, so sanctifying are its effects and wide-ranging its blessings.

Those people who are prevented by circumstances from spending a full hour in adoration are nonetheless encouraged to spend shorter periods of time before the Lord. So one could quite legitimately speak of a Holy Half-Hour, or even a Holy Few Minutes. St. Catherine of Genoa has said the last word on the subject: "Any time spent before the Eucharistic presence, be it long or short, is the best-spent time of our lives."

The Reparation Motive

Making reparation for one's own sins and those of others attaches closely to the Holy Hour in keeping with Our Lord's Gethsemane request. Thus we become closely united as co-victims with the Lamb of God taking upon himself the world's sins during his agony.

Young Francisco Marto, the Fatima seer mentioned earlier, spent long hours kneeling before the Lord, simply repeating the prayer taught them by the angel:

> My God, I believe, I adore, I trust, I love you. I ask pardon for those who do not believe, do not adore, do not trust, do not love you.[21]

It was likewise in a spirit of reparation that St. Francis of Assisi would repeatedly ask the God-Man during his night-long vigils to spread his love to those many hearts that did not love him. Similarly Charles de Foucauld devoted hours on end simply to consoling the Eucharistic Heart of Jesus wounded by the world's sins.

Adoration Petition and Miracle

The prayer of petition, too, can predominate during our times of adoration. A striking instance of this was the urgent night-long request made to the Eucharistic Lord by the community of nuns (Missionary Sisters of the Sacred Heart), plus some lay nurses, at Columbus Hospital in New York. It had been founded just a few years previously by Mother Frances Xavier Cabrini.

Earlier that day (March 14, 1921) a new-born baby boy had been the victim of a dreadful error in the maternity ward. The nurse rinsing his eyes inadvertently used a heavily under-diluted solution of silver nitrate, with the result that the baby's eyes were completely destroyed.

This prompted the community to spend the entire night begging the Eucharistic Heart of Jesus, through Mother Cabrini's intercession, to perform a miracle. And He did. The following morning the baby was found to have a new pair of beautiful blue eyes. This was vouched for by a whole body of medical authorities.

Indeed, that miracle was later accepted by the Vatican in Mother Cabrini's beatification process. Happily one of the special guests at the ceremony in Rome was the baby involved—Peter Smith, by now a fine young man in his late teens. He later became a priest and worked in a Texas diocese.

Praise and Adoration

To offer praise and worship to the Incarnate Word was the main motive that fired many illustrious devotees of adoration to be generous and self-sacrificing to a degree. This extract from Charles de Foucauld's diary exemplifies their spirit:

> What a tremendous delight, my God, to spend over 15 hours with nothing else to do but look at you and say, "Lord, I love you." Oh, what sweet delight!

Numerous other examples are on record, each of them a powerful spur for our own mediocre selves; they make us realize how much we need the starlight of heroic sanctity. St. Margaret

Mary once spent 14 hours in uninterrupted adoration. In the case of St. Aloysius Gonzaga, so long and motionless did he habitually kneel before the tabernacle that an artist had ample time to capture him on canvas.

St. Benedict Joseph Labre was known to kneel in the same position for eight hours or more in the Eucharistic presence. And, finally, St. Frances Xavier Cabrini on one occasion remained 12 continuous hours completely absorbed in adoration of the Eucharistic Heart of Jesus.

Eucharist and Gospel

A valuable method of prayer recommended by St. Peter Eymard is that we consider the various Gospel episodes in the light of the Eucharist, which he likened to "a divine prism through which all these mysteries can be studied."[22]

The saint went on to suggest a practical way of going about this during Eucharistic adoration. You select any gospel episode and as it were project it, stage it, around the sacramental Jesus before you.

The important thing is that you make yourself an active participant in the story, not just a spectator. This can be combined with something St. Ignatius proposes: with the eyes and ears of imagination, see and hear what Jesus and the persons concerned are doing and saying. Always remember, St. Ignatius adds, that what Jesus is saying and doing is *for you personally*; that is, for love of you and for your eternal salvation. Therefore speak intimately and confidently to him from your heart and, if devotion so moves you, also to those featured with him in the gospel story.

Putting This into Practice

Let us now apply this technique to some sample gospel scenarios; each can be developed as personal devotion may suggest. Remember that this same method can be equally applied to every gospel episode; so choose your own particular favourites.

1. **The Bethlehem Scene (Lk. 1:41–2:16)**

   Bethlehem means literally "the house of bread." The Blessed Sacrament makes each church a house of the living bread. The tabernacle is his crib. Mary, Joseph and the angels worship Jesus herein. And so do we—the Wise Men and Women guided here by the star of faith. Like our original counterparts we must adore him and offer our gifts: the gold of our homage, the frankincense of our prayer, the myrrh of our sufferings. Ask him in return for your heart's desire. And make the same request through his mother and St. Joseph.

2. **The Presentation in the Temple (Lk. 2:22–38)**

   Ask Mary to put her Infant Son into your arms as she did for Simeon—and as the priest gives him to you in Holy Communion. Petition Jesus to give you a Simeon-like faith in his divinity. Also ask Mary to bring you closer to her as the Mother of Sorrows.

3. **Nazareth (Lk. 2:39–52)**

   Here, with the Holy Family, we are in a most advanced school of Christian holiness. Ask the Eucharistic Jesus, his mother and St. Joseph in turn to help you progress in the ways of the Lord—faith, hope, charity, patience, kindness, peace, purity, etc. And beg them, too, to strengthen your prayer-life. Pray particularly for your domestic and family needs.

4. **Call of the First Disciples (Jn. 1:35–40)**

   John and Andrew asked Jesus where he lived. "Come and see," He replied. "And they remained with him the rest of that day." We "come and see" him in his Eucharistic dwelling-place. And we must stay faithfully with him during life's long day until the night of death. His "come and see" invitation applies chiefly and ultimately to the beatific vision; we shall see and enjoy him everlastingly as He is.

5. **Jacob's Well (Jn. 4:3–42)**

   The tabernacle is the deep well of grace. Here Jesus awaits us. "If we but knew the gift of God"—namely, the Eucharistic presence, the Author of grace himself, the Source of the living waters that spring up to eternal life. Ask St. Photina (alias the Samaritan Woman) to intercede that your Eucharistic worship in spirit and in truth may grow ever stronger and purer.

6. **Bethany (Jn. 11:28)**

   The Master is really and truly present here in Eucharistic form; and He calls us, invites us, pleads with us, to come and adore him as did Mary, Martha and Lazarus. Ask these in turn to gain for you the grace of close intimacy with Jesus, their familiar Friend and yours.

7. **Calvary (Jn. 19:18–30)**

   The wounds of Jesus are now glorified in his Eucharistic Body. But this same Body is sacramentally sacrificed in every Mass. So we can meditate on the crucified Christ. The Mother of Sorrows is present, grieving over mankind's sins. Ask her to give you a horror of sin and a burning zeal for souls.

8. **The Ascension (Acts 1:9–14)**

   Offer Jesus your worship and congratulations on having consummated his lifework. Then follow Mary and the Apostles to the Upper Room, "where they with one mind gave themselves up to prayer" as they awaited the Spirit of Pentecost. Their prayer was also Eucharistic—in and through the "breaking of bread."

Perpetual Adoration

Here we come to the devotion which reflects as closely as is possible in this world the life of heaven. For, in that paradisal world, Mary, the paramount adorer of the most High God, together with the angels and saints, sings his praises perpetually. And to promote within the Church Militant a matching devotion towards him present in the Blessed Sacrament is Mary's very special wish and intention.

This is reflected in the fact that she makes perpetual adoration a key feature of her shrines, as is exemplified at Guadalupe, Lourdes, and Fatima. And in one of her Medjugorje messages (August 25, 1995) she specifically urged that perpetual adoration be implemented by parishes all over the world.

In so doing, the mother of the Blessed Sacrament was echoing almost to the letter the appeal made by John Paul II when, in 1982, he inaugurated perpetual adoration in a chapel of St. Peter's—and encouraged every single parish and religious community in the universal Church to do the same. This papal appeal was repeated at the Eucharistic Congress in Seville in 1993.

Perpetual adoration means exactly what it says: worship of the Blessed Sacrament, exposed or in the tabernacle, by a succession of voluntary adorers ("watchers," as they are called) continued without intermission by day and by night. It is essentially a lay activity; that is, once the go-ahead has been given by the parish clergy, it is parishioners as a rule that organize the recruitment of watchers, the drawing-up of rosters and schedules, the coordination of everyone and everything concerned.

The main concern is to ensure that each of the 168 hours of the week is covered by at least one watcher. Experience shows that, once the initial organization has been set up, perpetual adoration virtually runs itself.

Its Spiritual Benefits

So immense are its spiritual benefits that Pope St. Pius X hailed perpetual adoration as *the devotion which surpasses all others*. And Paul VI had it mainly in mind when he echoed the hope generated by Vatican II that a new era of Eucharistic piety would pervade the whole Church.[23]

As we would expect, an outstanding spiritual growth and impetus tend to spring from perpetual adoration. It brings heaven's choice blessings in the first place on those generous souls that keep their hour-long tryst with the Lord. But, being such a powerhouse of grace, the devotion extends its influence far beyond the individual adorers, touching their homes and families and reaching out to the parish community and beyond.

Nor is this to be wondered at. He who came to cast on earth the fire of divine love is mysteriously yet really present before the eyes of faith; and He rewards our loving adoration by spreading far and wide throughout the world those sacred flames kindled within the tabernacle—as St. Catherine of Siena was once privileged to witness.

The Graces of Perpetual Adoration

Our Eucharistic faith tells us that Christ the King is himself here present, the tabernacle serving equivalently as his throne of grace. In this context, then, we may aptly apply the inspired and inspiring words: "Let us come boldly before the throne of grace, to meet with mercy and win that grace which will help us in our needs" (Heb. 4:16).

The graces to be won through perpetual adoration are manifold. At the personal level, each individual watcher's hour-long vigil before the throne of grace strengthens their faith and invigorates their overall spiritual life. At the parish level, its benefits and fruits are commonly seen in an increased Mass attendance; a fair number of lapsed parishioners return to the practice of the faith; Confessions tend to go up in numbers; marital and family problems are in not a few cases eased, if not fully solved; and vocations to the priesthood and religious life often owe their origins to this source.

One of perpetual adoration's most ardent advocates was Mother Teresa, who sent this special message to her far-flung friends and supporters:

> When you look at the crucifix, you understand how much Jesus loved you. When you look at the sacred Host, you understand how much Jesus loves you now. This is why you should ask your parish priest to have perpetual adoration in your parish. I beg the Blessed Mother to touch the hearts of all parish priests that they may have perpetual adoration in their parishes, and that it will spread throughout the whole world.

The literally Church-wide and worldwide benefits that flow from the apostolate of Eucharistic prayer have been highlighted by the Holy Father. Many present-day evils, he assures us, could be eliminated through its dynamic power. He goes on:

> The Church and the world have great need of Eucharistic adoration. Jesus waits for us in this sacrament of love. Let us be generous with our time in going to meet him in adoration and contemplation full of faith. And let us be ready to make reparation for the great faults and crimes of the world. May our adoration never cease.[24]

Increase of Vocations

To return now to an all-important fruit of perpetual adoration mentioned a little earlier: the kindling of vocations to the priesthood and religious life. Archbishop Elden Curtiss of Omaha, Nebraska, has testified that the seminaries in the U.S.A. blessed with significantly higher numbers of candidates are precisely those within dioceses where Eucharistic adoration is more widely practised. Similarly Paul Augustin Cardinal Mayer reports that in Holland, where the drop in priestly vocations has been drastic, the seminary in one particular diocese whose bishop recently started promoting perpetual adoration now has something like 60 students.[25]

These remarkable results have been paralleled in Ireland by the experience of Bishop Seamus Hegarty, who was instrumental in setting up widespread perpetual adoration in the diocese of

Raphoe. He is on record as saying that in 1990 the annual intake of students for his diocesan seminary had risen to 20. And of these *all but one* came from parishes where perpetual adoration is practised.

As regards promoting vocations to religious life, Mother Teresa, addressing a meeting of religious in May 1988, recommended Eucharistic adoration as a powerful means to this end. Her own Sisters of Charity, she pointed out, had doubled their numbers since adopting the devotion.

Adoration and Spiritual Communion

By spiritual communion is meant the earnest desire to receive Holy Communion and its fruits when sacramental reception is not licit or possible. St. Thomas teaches that fervent spiritual communions can produce as much, if not more, grace than is the case with sacramental Communion; all depends on the subjective dispositions of the communicant.[26]

No wonder, then, that so many eminent spiritual guides, including Saints Teresa of Ávila and Francis of Sales, encourage us to practise spiritual communion. Frequently to invite the Lord of the Eucharist to enter spiritually under our roof—few have preached and practised this more ardently than Blessed Peter Faber, one of St. Ignatius's first companions. He saw clearly how effectively it rekindles the grace of past Holy Communions and prepares us to receive the sacrament more worthily in the future.

Our Lady's Spiritual Communions

The lives of God's holy ones are replete with examples of spiritual communing—ardent, yearning, and virtually uninterrupted—with the Eucharistic Lord. But none could possibly compare in this regard with the Lord's mother. St. Peter Eymard says of her:

> The Eucharist had so powerful an attraction for the Blessed Virgin that she could not live away from it. She lived in it and by it. She passed her days and her nights at the feet of her divine Son.... Her love for

> her hidden God shone in her countenance and communicated its ardour to all about her.[27]

In a word, Mary was the spiritual communicant *par excellence*. During the years she spent awaiting her call to join the Saviour in heavenly glory, Mary's faith feasted on her uninterrupted spiritual communion with him between sacramental Communions.

Now, as mother of the Eucharist, she can help us to make maximum use of spiritual communion—this precious privilege within our power, this pearl among devotions.

With a Fling of the Heart

The priest-poet, Gerard Manley Hopkins, wrote one of his masterpieces as a tribute to five Franciscan nuns drowned in a shipwreck off the English coast in 1875. As death drew near, these brave women, schooled in familiar converse with the God of the Eucharist, now united themselves with him present in multiple tabernacles across the world. Hopkins has one of them say:

> I whirled out wings that spell
> And fled with a fling of the heart
> to the heart of the Host.[28]

Here we have a dramatic illustration of Eucharistic faith reaching out effortlessly and unerringly to that loving Person reserved in our churches. We also see here a striking example of Eucharistic faith homing in, so to speak, on the tabernacle from some considerable distance away.

From Anywhere and Everywhere

One valuable lesson contained in this example is that distance is no barrier to Eucharistic faith and adoration. For God's heavenly kingdom, the Eucharist included, transcends our spatio-temporal limitations. So we can effectively adore the Word-made-Host wherever we may happen to be, and at any time of the day or night.

In fact, so dynamic is Eucharistic faith that it is well able to wing its way "with a fling of the heart to the heart of the Host" from literally anywhere and everywhere. This applies equally to a sinking ship or an airliner cruising at high altitude; a factory floor or from behind a steering wheel; a crowded shopping area or a country lane; a classroom or a prison cell; a kitchen or a hospital ward; a train compartment or a sickbed—all locations are in reality equidistant from the tabernacle.

This helps us to realize how amazingly easy, unrestricted and instantaneous is access to the sacramental Saviour. At whatever distance we may find ourselves relative to the tabernacle, He is just a thought, just a fling of the heart, away; and our adoration and spiritual communions register with him as effectively as if we were physically in his presence.

The Garabandal story supplies us with an interesting case in point. When the diocesan authorities declared the church out of bounds for the young visionaries during their ecstatic apparitions, Our Lady enjoined them to comply strictly with this ruling. Very pointedly, though, she had them walk around the church building several times while directing their devotions to the Blessed Sacrament within.

A Shining Example

Earlier mention of Eucharistic adoration from a sickbed brings to mind the inspiring life of Alexandrina da Costa, who died on October 13, 1955, aged 51. For long years this Portuguese mystic was totally bedridden and in severe pain, the result of a spinal injury sustained in her teens. And till the end of her days she was destined to be a victim-soul, offering generously and joyously her continuous sufferings in union with our Lord's.

Thanks to her devotion to Our Lady of Fatima, Alexandrina had been rewarded early on with a grace that would add a whole new dimension to her life. As her thoughts strayed one day to the nearby church, she suddenly realized, vividly and unforgettably, that Jesus in its tabernacle was also, like herself, a shut-in, a prisoner. And the further realization struck her that she could adore and commune directly with him there, on a heart-to-heart basis, from her little room—"that great altar of sacrifice," as Cardinal Cerejeira was later to describe it.

This new-found Eucharistic awareness lit up the horizons of her young life, inspiring her to unite herself thenceforward, in the company of Mary, with the tabernacled Lover of Souls. There she kept watch with unceasing love and self-immolation, consoling his wounded Eucharistic Heart, and winning thereby the precious grace of conversion for sinners. Alexandrina has been declared a Servant of God, and numerous favours have already been granted through her intercession.

Another Shining Example

Also on the road to eventual beatification is Anna Schaeffer, a woman in southern Germany, the circumstances of whose life and Eucharist-oriented spirituality compare broadly with those of Alexandrina da Costa. She died on October 13, 1925, aged 47.

In her late teens Anna sustained terrible burns in an accident, suffering from them incessantly and condemned to be bed-bound for the remainder of her days. Closely guided and consoled by Our Lady, she came to realize that her vocation was to be a victim-soul, filling up in her poor broken body, for the salvation of sinners, what is lacking in the sufferings of Christ (cf. Col. 1:24).

The mother of the Eucharist further won for her generous daughter the signal grace of making that tabernacled presence in the nearby church the focus, the magnetic centre, of her waking moments. With many a fling of her heart Anna sped to that divine Heart burning with love of us in the Host. And sleepless night after sleepless night she would spend in spirit before the tabernacle alongside her beloved Mother of Sorrows, jointly adoring with her the God whose glorious wounds testify to his love.

Indeed, Anna came to share in those five sacred wounds in a literal way: she received the stigmata at the age of 28. Like her Portuguese counterpart, Anna Schaeffer has already won thousands of favours for those who invoke her intercession.

The Heart of Our Churches

One favour we should ask of these two shining stars of Eucharistic adoration is that we may come to value it more deeply and practise it more assiduously. "Give him your heart a thousand times a day." St. Francis of Sales is here equivalently counselling us to cast many a fling of our heart to the heart of the Host.

That sacred Host, as Paul VI states in his *Credo*, is "the beating heart" of every church. Or to quote John Paul II:

> In the tabernacle of each church we possess a shining beacon, through contact with which our lives may be illuminated and transformed.[29]

Next we consider Mary's intimate role within the Eucharist as it relates to the Trinity.

---

[1] St. Peter Julian Eymard: IN THE LIGHT OF THE MONSTRANCE: Edited by Charles DeKeyser, S.S.S., (Cleveland) 1947
[2] Frederick William Faber: THE SPIRIT OF FR. FABER: The Blessed Sacrament. (London) 1914
[3] Council of Trent: DENZINGER, #642, #1656
[4] Pope Paul VI: MYSTERIUM FIDEI, 56-57
[5] Pope John Paul II: INAESTIMABILE DONUM, 20
[6] Pope John Paul II: LETTER TO THE BISHOP OF LIÈGE (Reported in *L'Osserv. Romano*, 26 June 1996)
[7] Joseph Cardinal Ratzinger: THE RATZINGER REPORT, (Leominster) 1985
[8] Pope John Paul II: Homily at INTERNATIONAL EUCHARISTIC CONGRESS, Seville, 1993, (Reported in *L'Osserv. Romano*, 23 June 1993)
[9] St. Alphonsus Liguori: THE HOLY EUCHARIST: VISITS TO THE BLESSED SACRAMENT: Third Visit, (Brooklyn) 1934
[10] St. Peter Julian Eymard: loc. cit.
[11] The Marian Movement of Priests: TO THE PRIESTS, OUR LADY'S BELOVED SONS (11th Edit. 1995): Message given on 21 August 1987, 430
[12] Blessed M. Faustina Kowalska: DIVINE MERCY IN MY SOUL: Diary (1987), 80
[13] F. Sanchez-Ventura y Pascual: THE APPARITIONS OF GARABANDAL, (Detroit), 1981, 181
[14] Pope John XXIII: JOURNAL OF A SOUL, (London) 1965
[15] Pope John Paul II: ADDRESS IN PHOENIX PARK, Dublin, 29 September 1979
[16] St. Alphonsus Liguori: op. cit. Eighth Visit
[17] Karl Rahner, S.J.: EUCHARISTIC WORSHIP: THEOLOGICAL INVESTIGATIONS, 23, (London), 1992, 114

[18] Professor A. O'Rahilly: FATHER WILLIAM DOYLE, S.J.: A SPIRITUAL STUDY. (London) 1930, 210
[19] Sr. Briege McKenna, O.S.C: MIRACLES DO HAPPEN (Michigan) 1987, 25
[20] Pope John XXIII: loc. cit.
[21] John M. Haffert: HER OWN WORDS: THE MEMOIRS OF SISTER LUCIA (101 Foundation), 1993, 80
[22] St. Peter Julian Eymard: loc. cit.
[23] Pope Paul VI: MYSTERIUM FIDEI, 13
[24] Pope John Paul II: DOMINICAE COENAE: Letter to Priests, Holy Thursday, 1980
[25] INSIDE THE VATICAN: An Interview with Paul Augustin Cardinal Mayer, O.S.B. (September 1996)
[26] St. Thomas Aquinas: SUMMA THEOLOGICA, Pars 3, q.80, a.I
[27] St. Peter Julian Eymard: loc. cit.
[28] Gerard Manley Hopkins: POEMS AND PROSE. Selected by W. H. Gardner: The Wreck of the Deutschland, (Penguin), 1966
[29] Pope John Paul II: HOMILY AT EUCHARISTIC CONGRESS, Seville 1993 (Reported in *L'Osserv. Romano*, 23 June 1993)

CHAPTER SIX

Mary, Eucharist, Trinity

Pope Paul VI spoke for all Catholic tradition when he said of Mary that she comprehends better than any other creature, including the highest angels, the immensity of God's Eucharistic gift.[1]

The immensity of this gift consists essentially, of course, in its being the actual living reality of the Second Person of the Trinity, sacramentally present among us as Priest, Victim, and spiritual Food. And the immensity of God's Eucharistic gift is further enhanced by bringing with it myriad attendant co-presences—angels and human spirits alike. This glorious company, along with heaven's queen, perpetually behold and adore the glorified Christ truly with us in the consecrated Host, albeit concealed from mortal eyes behind the faith-curtain.

But that is not all. The Eucharistic gift assumes even more awesome proportions when we reflect that the Son of God present herein is ever united, intimately and indivisibly, with his co-Persons in the Trinity—his Eternal Father and their mutual Spirit of Love; which means that they, too, are mysteriously yet really with him, and consequently with us no less. In effect, then, the total Eucharistic mystery includes the presence of both the Father and the Holy Spirit as an inseparable concomitant. That is, the Blessed Sacrament embraces the Trinitarian mystery within its compass.

Again, it is Mary who comprehends most clearly of all this vital connection between her Son's Eucharistic life and his two fellow-Persons in the Godhead. And she does so because, in addition to being mother of God the Son, Mary, as Vatican II noted, is "the most loved daughter of the Father and the sanctuary of the Holy Spirit."[2]

Less Familiar Territory

For many readers, including well-instructed ones, this Trinitarian perspective on the Eucharist is likely to be relatively unfamiliar territory. The reason is that God's threefold personality and the sacramental role of the Son have become rigidly compartmentalized and virtually isolated from each other in theological textbooks and devotional writing.

Now this is plainly a pity and an impoverishment, seeing that God's triunity is bound to enrich our understanding of the Word's Eucharistic life and role. At the same time, it is equally bound to expand the horizons of our Eucharistic devotion and lend it an added depth and warmth.

Clearly, then, it is to her who is invoked both as mother of the Eucharist and favoured shrine of the Trinity that we should turn for light and guidance on the Blessed Sacrament's vital relationship and close affinities with the Three-in-One.

The Incarnation Prolonged

Had the Eternal Word not become man, his Eucharistic existence would not have been possible. For this sacrament's whole meaning and purpose is to extend his incarnate presence to every possible place on earth in all succeeding generations. Of course, only the Second Person is corporeally present in the consecrated Host, He alone having been made flesh; as for the Father and the Holy Spirit, they necessarily accompany him inasmuch as they are identical in being and Godhead with the Eternal Word.

Nor does the Word's sacramental role affect in the least his status—that is, his divine sonship and personhood—within the Trinity. He remains, now and forever, the Only-begotten Son of the Father, with whom He jointly outbreathes the Holy Spirit as the expression of their mutual love. St. Paul leaves us in no doubt about this. "In Christ," he says, "the whole plenitude of deity is embodied, and dwells in him" (Col. 2:10).

It will become more and more evident as we proceed how profoundly interwoven the Eucharist is with the mystery of the three Selves in God—that sublime truth which Pope Leo XIII entitled "the fountainhead of all faith's mysteries."[3] Indeed, from the Trinity as from its source there streams illumination upon *all* revealed truths, just as from this same source flows every grace and gift making for our sanctification and salvation.

Trinity in Itself

It is only to be expected that Trinitarian doctrine should cast its own floodlight on Eucharistic faith and devotion. For the substance and inner life of the Godhead, as the mother of the Word Incarnate knows so well, is identical with her Eucharistic Son's. It will prove helpful, therefore, if beforehand we briefly recall what we believe concerning the Trinity as such—that primordial master-truth which holds pride of place in our Creed. We shall see that the Trinitarian mystery feeds into our understanding of the Blessed Sacrament, besides helping to kindle and deepen our Eucharistic devotion.

Revelation tells us that in the one, eternal God there exist three separate Persons. Co-equal and co-eternal, they are united, bonded together, in the single Godhead, the selfsame substance, the one common essence. Each person is fully God; yet they jointly possess the Godhead's identical being, nature, mind and will. Moreover, all God's activities and operations flow from the unitary divine nature, though we conveniently appropriate to each Person certain specific functions, such as creation to the Father and sanctification to the Holy Spirit.

The only difference of any kind between the three Persons is in their respective relations of origin. Indeed, it is these relations that as it were constitute each of the divine trio in existence. Thus the first Person is constituted by his Fatherhood, the second by his Sonship, the third by his procession as the Living Love reciprocated between Father and Offspring acting as a joint principle.

God the Father is the principle without principle, the source-Person from whom the others proceed. Of these processions the first arises as follows. From all eternity the Father's infinite mind conceives a thought, which is the perfect image of himself and his divine perfections. So perfect indeed is this thought that it is alive with the Thinker's own divine life; that is, it possesses his full being and mirrors his glory and majesty. This living, infinite thought we call the Father's Word, the Offspring of his mind; it is his Only-begotten Son, the Wisdom-Person in the Trinity.

The next Trinitarian procession is that of the Holy Spirit. He is the Love-Person, so called because He originates as the love breathed out towards each other reciprocally by Father and Son. The Holy Spirit literally personifies their mutual love and self-gift to each other.

Trinity in Eucharist

Our faith further proclaims that the undivided Trinity was and remains wholly present in the Word-made-Flesh. And exactly the same holds true of the Word-made-Eucharist. As Fr. Michael O'Carroll says apropos of the Lord's sacramental presence:

> At this centre of supernatural life the soul meets the Holy Trinity in the most profound way. The encounter is not a pious figment. It takes its meaning from the full reality of the God-Man and the import of his Incarnation for revelation, for the redemption and renewal of mankind, in every phase of existence, personal and collective.[4]

A key word in Trinitarian theology is immanence. It expresses the intimate sharing of the identical divine life by the trio of Persons; so undividedly united, in fact, are the Three that they remain wholly present within each other in an eternal communion of life, love and activity. The technical term for this mutual indwelling or interpenetration of divine Persons is circuminsession; it means that each is not only fully present to the others but subsists within them.

How this indwelling arises becomes clearer when we consider their relations of origin. The Word is the Father's thought or self-reflection, generated in his mind from endless ages. Hence Thinker and Thought are vitally and inseparably united in that boundless process of knowing and being known.

Similarly, the procession of the Third Person as the living personification of the Father-Son exchange of love entails that He is ever present within his source; which source is in turn the object of his return-love, namely, the Eternal Father and his beloved Son.

Finally, these two processions within the Trinity are not to be understood as indicating a static or fixed-state reality; rather, the processions are perpetually ongoing, the Father ever generating his Son, and their mutual love issuing eternally as the Third Person. This reciprocal process between Persons brings about within the Trinity a dynamic circulation of life and love.

Hence Trinitarian inter-relations are infinitely more than a mere close fellowship or communitarian living. The Three are irresistibly drawn towards each other in an unending exchange of identical divinity, of total understanding, of mutual love, and of eternal self-giving.

Trinity Indwells Eucharist

Clearly the Mass, Holy Communion and adoration of the Blessed Sacrament take on rich and exciting new perspectives in this Trinitarian light. It enables the eyes of faith to discern that the God-Man's Eucharistic presence is at the same time the all-privileged *locus*, the sacred shrine, wherein the all-holy Threefold are enthroned and their inner life is perpetuated.

Christ's words to the apostle Philip apply to his Eucharistic self as relevantly as they did during his mortal life:

> Philip, have I been with you so long and yet you do not know me? He who has seen me has seen the Father; so how can you say, "Show us the Father"? Do you not believe that I am in the Father and the Father in me? The words that I say to you I do not speak on my own authority; but the Father who dwells in me does his works. Believe me that I am in the Father and the Father in me.... I pray that they

> all may be one, even as thou, Father, art in me, and I in thee, that they also may be in us, so that the world may believe that thou hast sent me.[5]

The reciprocal indwelling of the Holy Spirit in the Father and the Son is likewise part of the Eucharistic mystery. St. Paul has supplied us with a text implying this doctrine:

> There is no depth in God's nature so deep that the Spirit cannot find it out. Who else can know a man's thoughts, except the man's own spirit that is within him? So no one else can know God's thoughts, but the Spirit of God.[6]

Trinity and Eucharistic Liturgy

> The worship given to the Trinity of Father, Son and Holy Spirit above all accompanies and permeates the celebration of the Eucharistic liturgy.[7]

This papal teaching is verified in the Mass right from the opening Sign of the Cross until the final blessing, both of which are performed with the Trinitarian formula. Indeed, throughout the Mass's entire framework, in prayer after prayer, the three divine Persons are jointly or singly invoked.

At the outset the celebrant prays that all present may be filled with "the grace of our Lord Jesus Christ, the love of God, and the fellowship of the Holy Spirit." This testifies to our belief that in the sacrament of the altar "the true God is one in Trinity and a Trinity in one."[8]

The threefold *Kyrie*, St. Thomas explains, besides being an acknowledgement of our human ignorance, guilt and deserved punishment for sin, also "signifies that the three divine Persons are within one another."[9]

The *Glory Be* prayer and the longer *Gloria*—the so-called doxologies—both proclaim the same belief. As for the Eucharistic Prayers, they are deeply impregnated with the mystery of the three Persons co-active in the sacramental presence and its sanctifying effects. For example, the second of these Prayers opens with the words:

> Lord, you are holy indeed, the fountain of all holiness. Let your Spirit come upon these gifts to make them holy, so that they may become for us the body and blood of our Lord Jesus Christ.

Once these gifts have been consecrated into the body and blood of Christ, his incarnate life is thus renewed and his redemptive mission continued. But his co-Persons in the Trinity do not—because they cannot—separate themselves from him in his new mode of existence as the Christ of the Eucharist.

Never, therefore, is the Eternal Word on his own. Through the mutual indwelling common to the Three, the whole Trinitarian life is immanent within the consecrated elements. And within those elements the Son of God continues his essential mission of leading us to his Father and ours. Thus through the Son's sacramental presence we have direct access both to God the Father and the Love-Person they co-originate.

Mystical Experiences

Many mystics in Church history have been privileged to experience in some sort the co-presence of the Trinity within the context of the Mass. A notable example was St. Ignatius Loyola, whose spiritual diary makes frequent mention of such experiences; they sometimes went hand-in-hand with similar ones bearing on the mother of the Eucharist—as we saw in an earlier chapter.

So illuminating were his mystical intuitions of the Trinity during the Eucharistic celebration, said Ignatius, that he could not have learned as much about the subject even if he had devoted thereto a lifetime of study. Here is an extract from his writings:

> During Mass the tears were more copious than the previous day and lasted continuously.... I knew or felt or saw, God knows, that, on speaking to the Father and seeing that He was one Person of the Blessed Trinity, I felt moved to love all the Trinity,

> especially as the other Persons were all in the Trinity by their very essence: the same feeling when I prayed to the Son and to the Holy Spirit; when I felt consolation I was delighted with any one of them, and I rejoiced in acknowledging it as coming from all Three.[10]

Trinity and Holy Communion

Besides being a sacred banquet for our human spirits, Holy Communion presents us with a feast of faith and devotion. For in receiving the bread of heaven our unworthy selves play host not just to one but three divine Guests—the Incarnate Word together with his indwelling, and therefore ever-concomitant and ever-present, fellow-Persons in the Godhead.

Again, no one understands this profound mystery more clearly than the Blessed Virgin. At the Annunciation she received the three Persons in what was effectively the first-ever and inaugural Holy Communion. The Holy Spirit came down upon her; the power of the most high Father overshadowed her; and the Word was conceived as a human embryo in her womb (cf. Lk. 1:35). After the Word's eventual Ascension into heaven, Mary regularly received his Eucharistic Self, in whom she knew to greet and adore not only her Son but also his eternal Father and their Living Love. Accordingly she progressively became ever more perfectly the shrine of the triune God.

Because of the three Persons' oneness of being and reciprocal interiority, we receive in sacramental Communion the generated Son and the concomitant Presence of his Father-genitor. By this same token the Holy Spirit proceeding from them both is also received. Scheeben said in this connection:

> Since the Holy Spirit, the Spirit of the Son, is really united to the Son's body, in which He reposes and dwells, He also comes to us.... In the body of the Word, which is filled with the Holy Spirit, we receive the Holy Spirit himself, as it were from the

> breast and heart of the Word whence He proceeds.[11]

The Trinity's Life within Us

Again the experience of the mystics throws much light on the amazing mystery of the Trinity's co-Presence in the consecrated elements. Prominent among them was St. Catherine of Siena; in poetic strain she wrote:

> O Trinity, eternal Trinity! Fire, abyss of love...
> Was it necessary that you should give
> Even the Holy Trinity as food for souls?...
> You gave us not only your Word
> Through the Redemption and in the Eucharist,
> But you also gave yourself
> In your fullness of love for your creature.[12]

St. Elizabeth of the Trinity was another mystic to be caught up into this profound experience. One of her most illuminating insights was that our Holy Communions are essentially a participation in the Son's eternal communion with his Father. Our Lord himself alluded to this when He said, "As I live by the Father, so he that eats me will also live by me" (Jn. 6:57).

Another truth underlined by St. Elizabeth is that in Holy Communion we partake not only of Christ's body and blood but of the Trinity's inmost life. That is, we commune with all three Persons. Our technical word for this participation is sanctifying grace. And sanctifying grace stands, in the first place, for the actual indwelling of the Trinity in the soul. Our Lord referred to this when He said of anyone remaining true to his word: "He will win my Father's love, and we will both come to him and make our continual abode with him" (Jn. 14:23). Our reception of Holy Communion therefore serves to deepen and consolidate the divine inhabitation within the soul and nourishes the life of grace.

It was through her special devotion to Mary under the title of *Janua Coeli*—Gate of Heaven—that St. Elizabeth came to have such an intense devotion to the three divine Indwellers present within her through grace and coming to her through sacramental

Communion. Early on in religious life she made this resolution:

> I will unite myself with the soul of the Blessed Virgin when the Father overshadowed her, the Son took flesh in her, and the Holy Spirit descended to work the great mystery. The Holy Trinity is active; it gives itself, pours itself into her. What would we be living for in Carmel if we were not likewise enveloped by the divine?[13]

Mary and the Three Countenances

Pope John Paul II has reminded us that devotion to Mary, besides being oriented towards her Son, is *even more profoundly* rooted in the Trinity.[14] Similarly von Balthasar hails the mother of God as the archetype and model of those who contemplate the Three-in-One mystery as being "objectified and concretely visible" in the humanity of her Son. By giving him that humanity, his mother caused "the mystery of the Three Countenances" to shine out upon our world.[15]

So let us often reflect with Mary that it is these Three Countenances which gaze out lovingly at us from the tabernacle. And the God-Man's words now resonate with an added relevance when applied to the Blessed Sacrament: "He who sent me is with me; He has not left me alone" (Jn. 8:29).

Nor is that all. The Father, besides being present along with his Word-Wisdom in the sacred Host, continues to beget him there. At the same time, the Begetter and the Begotten within the Host jointly and ceaselessly communicate the fullness of their life and being to the third divine Self who proceeds as the expression, the gift, the joy, of their shared love.

One of the great minds of Christian antiquity, St. Gregory Nazianzen, coined a formula which applies directly to the Word Incarnate dwelling among us sacramentally: "Eternal Wisdom became man in our midst in order to say to every one of us: 'Go to the Trinity!'"[16]

This was echoed by Our Lady of Fatima when she gave a clear indication that the Blessed Sacrament should be seen and adored in its true Trinitarian framework; thus in her first apparition she urged the seers to fall on their knees and say:

> O most holy Trinity, I adore you. My God, my God, I love you in the most Blessed Sacrament.[17]

Earlier the Angel of Peace in his third apparition to the Fatima seers had instructed them to say the following prayer, which similarly links the Eucharistic and Trinitarian mysteries:

> Most Holy Trinity, Father, Son and Holy Spirit, I adore you profoundly. I offer you the most precious body, blood, soul and divinity of Our Lord Jesus Christ present in all the tabernacles of the world....

Another vivid reminder of the Trinity's enthronement in the Blessed Sacrament is seen in St. Thomas's two Eucharistic hymns. In each he hails the three Persons enshrined in the divine bread which comes down from heaven. To quote the second verse of the *Tantum Ergo*:

> Glory be to God the Father;
> Praise to his co-equal Son;
> Adoration to the Spirit,
> Bond of love, in Godhead one.

Father of the Eucharist

Because the three Selves in the Godhead are a perfect unity, to adore one is to adore all three. Nonetheless we can and do address each of them individually, especially when we appropriate to one or the other certain qualities or roles. Never should we forget that each Person is a quite distinct and individual Self with whom we can dialogue just as we do with human individuals. This practice fits very well into our Eucharistic devotions, and can be especially helpful during adoration.

To begin with God the Father. He it is who gives us this precious gift of his Son in the first place, presenting us therein with what Balthasar calls "a concrete vision of the life of the

Trinity"[18] and so affording us easy and instant access to each of the Persons. With all the more reason, then, we should praise and thank the Father for being the living source and giver of Emmanuel-made-Eucharist, and for subsisting within him in this great sacrament of love.

Our adoration of the Father, as St. Elizabeth of the Trinity emphasizes,[19] is really a participation in the adoration made to him by the Man-God, who thus exemplifies all true human adorers of the Father in spirit and in truth (cf. Jn. 4:23). Indeed, von Balthasar describes the Word-made-flesh as "the Father's substantial Eucharist,"[20] that is, the perfect Thanksgiver who eternally offers back to the Father—in the Holy Spirit, with gratitude and love—the divine being and perfections He receives from him as his Progenitor.

No one could fail to see how nourishing it is for our faith and devotion to commune with God the Father, especially in the presence of the Eucharist. An easy and helpful devotion for those occasions—it is strongly recommended by St. Teresa of Ávila, among others—is to pray the *Our Father*. She advises us to do so slowly and unhurriedly, taking it phrase by phrase, even word by word, only moving on to the next when we have sipped to our satisfaction the contents of the preceding.

Holy Spirit and the Eucharist

To the Third Person we appropriate the fashioning of the Word's humanity in the womb of the Virgin Mary. Through this action the Second of the three Someones in God became literally a Some*body*. And when that Some*body* is transubstantiated into the Eucharist, we again appropriate the operation to the Love-Person who eternally unites him with the Father.

Indeed, St. Augustine points out, the Holy Spirit's function is not only to unite Father and Son but to draw us into union with them.[21] And our union with them means that we share, imperfectly in this world but consummately in the next, in their very own life, their joy, their delight, their happiness, their sweetness—all of which are personified in the Third Person.

As with prayer directed to the Father, so, too, when it is addressed to the Holy Spirit, a feast of faith and devotion beckons us, especially during adoration of the Blessed Sacrament. For the heart of Jesus beating there burns with love both divine and human—a love kindled within him by the Third Person. And his Eucharistic Heart is closely united with the Immaculate Heart of his mother—that masterpiece of the Holy Spirit.

The intimately close and ongoing relationship between God the Holy Spirit and his chosen spouse was underlined by the distinguished Russian Orthodox theologian, Bulgakov:

> The Holy Spirit does not at all leave her after the birth of Christ but remains forever in the full force of the Annunciation.... He abides in the ever-virgin Mary as in a holy temple, while her human personality seems to become transparent to him and provide him with a human countenance.[22]

St. Maximilian Kolbe, while always recognizing Mary's creaturely status, even went so far as to suggest the following bold analogy:

> This perfect union of the Immaculate One with the Holy Spirit makes her, in a certain manner of speaking, the Holy Spirit himself.... In a certain kind of way we can say that the Immaculate One is the incarnation of the Holy Spirit himself.[23]

Understanding and Piety

With Mary we adore the Holy Spirit whose earthly dwelling-place—rather, *in*dwelling-place—is the Eucharistic Saviour. Let us ask the Spirit of Jesus to increase his sevenfold gift within us, especially understanding and piety. For these bear in a special way on our union with the Three Persons subsisting within the Eucharistic reality.

The gift of understanding will help us to grasp more clearly the doctrine involved, though we shall never fully comprehend the Eucharist's mystery, let alone that of the Trinity. As for the gift of piety, it serves to kindle our faith, stir our charity, and warm our affections towards the God whose Threefold Countenance in the Host is the source and throne of grace.

Mention of "throne of grace" (cf. Heb. 4:16) conveniently cues us into our next consideration: the supernatural life of the Trinity. The hold-all label for this life is "grace." As will be seen, it comes to us in and from the Eucharistic Christ, and is universally mediated to us through his mother.

---

[1] Pope Paul VI: MYSTERIUM FIDEI, 65

[2] Vatican II: LUMEN GENTIUM, 53

[3] Pope Leo XIII: DIVINUM ILLUD MUNUS, AAS 29 (1896–7)

[4] Michael O'Carroll, C.S.Sp.: THEOTOKOS: THE EUCHARIST (Michael Glazier Inc.) 1982

[5] JN. 14:9–11; 17:20–21

[6] 1 COR. 2:10–11

[7] Pope John Paul II: DOMINICAE COENAE: Letter to Priests, Holy Thursday 1980

[8] OFFICE FOR THE FEAST OF THE HOLY TRINITY

[9] St. Thomas Aquinas: SUMMA THEOLOGICA, Pars 3, q.83, a.4

[10] ST. IGNATIUS LOYOLA: PERSONAL WRITINGS. Translated with Introduction by Joseph A. Munitiz, S.J. and Philip Endean, S.J. (Penguin Classics), 82–84

[11] M. J. Scheeben: THE MYSTERIES OF CHRISTIANITY. (London) 1954, VI, 26, 528

[12] St. Catherine of Siena: Quoted in ST. CATERINA DA SIENA, by G. Cavallini: Le Orazioni, Orazione 20

[13] Hans Urs von Balthasar: ELIZABETH OF DIJON. (London) 1956, 125–126

[14] Pope John Paul II: CROSSING THE THRESHOLD OF HOPE, (London) 1994, ch. 32

[15] Hans Urs von Balthasar: PRAYER: THE LIFE OF THE TRINITY (London), 1961, 154–156

[16] St. Gregory of Nazianzen: MORAL POEMS, PG 37, 913

[17] Francis Johnston: FATIMA, THE GREAT SIGN, (Rockford) 1979, 28, 35

[18] Hans Urs von Balthasar: loc. cit.

[19] Hans Urs von Balthasar: ELIZABETH OF DIJON, (London), 93–94

[20] Hans Urs von Balthasar: Quoted by John Saward in THE MYSTERIES OF MARCH: Balthasar on the Incarnation and Easter, (London) 1990, 98

[21] St. Augustine: DE TRINITATE, VII, 6. PL 43, 945

[22] Sergius Bulgakov: LE PARACLET (London), 1946, 238–239; 176–177

[23] St. Maximilian Kolbe: EPHMAR, 21 (1971) pp 231–232

CHAPTER SEVEN

Mary and Eucharistic Grace

A favourite insight of Pope Paul VI's was what he called "the atmosphere of grace that reigns about the Blessed Sacrament." And Pope John Paul II in turn has challenged us "to grow spiritually in the climate of the Holy Eucharist."[1]

Each statement affirms two key truths. First is that the Eucharistic Redeemer is the source of grace in all its fullness. Secondly, of his fullness, which can be likened almost to an atmosphere, a climate, a zone, a magnetic field centred upon and surrounding the tabernacle, we have all received—and should ever aspire to receive more and more (cf. Jn. 1:16).

Before going any further, we need to ask ourselves: what is the grassroots meaning of grace? What is its bottom line? Our Lord supplied the answer in declaring that his whole purpose in coming was that we might have *his divine life* within ourselves—and have it ever more abundantly (cf. Jn. 10:10). He now perpetuates his life-mission in and through the Eucharist, thus establishing it as the living source and centre of supernatural life. For this reason Vatican II hails the Blessed Sacrament as our chief treasure, our principal wealth. For contained therein is "the Church's whole spiritual good, namely, Christ himself ... the source and summit of the Christian life."[2]

The Eucharist is therefore absolutely central to the Church's life and apostolate. This was underlined in a message given by Mary through Fr. Stefano Gobbi:

> O Church, pilgrim and suffering, of which I am the

> Mother ... you must understand that the centre of your life, the fount of your grace, the source of your light, the principle of your apostolic action is found only here in the tabernacle where Jesus is truly kept. And Jesus is present to teach you how to grow, to help you go forward, to strengthen you in bearing witness, to give you courage in evangelizing, to support you in all your sufferings.[3]

Mother of the Eucharist

John Gerson was the first to apply the above title to Our Lady; he went on to address her as follows:

> You are the Mother of the Eucharist because you are the mother of grace. You, more than all others after your Son, were aware of this sacrament hidden from the ages.[4]

Mary is the full-of-grace woman, chosen and prepared by God to bear and bring up his Son, the world's Saviour. And our salvation was duly wrought by him through his sufferings and death. His mother shared coredemptively therein, meriting thereby her own appointment as mediatrix and intercessor of all graces.

Gerard Manley Hopkins says of her that she "mothers each new grace that does now reach our race." In the same poem he attributes to Mary the "atmosphere of grace" that Paul VI was later to associate with the Eucharist:

> I say that we are wound
> With mercy round and round
> As if with air: the same
> Is Mary ...
> Be thou, then, O thou dear
> Mother, my atmosphere:
> My happier world, wherein
> To wend and meet no sin.[5]

The Mother of the Eucharist ardently desires to share its

graces with us from her privileged position next to her Son's tabernacle-throne. She exhorts us in the words of Scripture:

> Let us come boldly, then, before the throne of grace, to meet with mercy, and win that grace which will help us in our needs.[6]

The Queen-Mother

The Blessed Virgin's status in heaven is that of Queen-Mother; as such she has instant access to the throne of the Most High and wields a tremendous power of intercession. We call this the "Marian prerogative." It was prefigured in Old Testament times in the special role and office attaching to the mothers of the great Davidic kings of Israel. Because these monarchs usually had multiple wives—a circumstance considered likely to cause problems of rank and precedence among them—the king's mother was chosen to be queen of the realm because of her intimate maternal relationship with him. Consequently the queen-mother became the most powerful advocate with her son on behalf of his subjects.

To give an example. A certain Israelite seeking a special favour from King Solomon was wise enough beforehand to approach Bethsabee, the queen-mother. "My request," he said, "is that thou wouldst say a word for me to king Solomon; there is nothing he can refuse thee." Bethsabee agreed to intervene on his behalf and made her way to the royal throne. The text continues:

> The king rose to meet her and bowed low; then he sat down on his throne again, and a throne was brought for her, the king's mother, to sit down at his right hand. "There is a light request that I would make of thee," she said; "pray do not disappoint me." "Make thy request, mother," he replied, "I will not turn a deaf ear to it."[7]

Mediatrix of All Graces

Mary's key role as channel of all graces flowing to mankind from the Eucharistic Saviour derives from her total sinlessness and divine motherhood.

In defining Mary's Immaculate Conception in 1854, Pius IX declared that the Creator adorned "the all-beautiful and perfect Virgin with an abundance of grace from the treasury of his Godhead."[8] Hereby she was prepared for her unique destiny as mother of the Word Incarnate. His human life began beneath her Immaculate Heart; there, too, was born the alliance of hearts which wrought our salvation.

This alliance is founded primarily on Christ's status and role as Redeemer. By freely consenting to give him his human body—the instrument of our redemption—Mary was already participating in her Son's destiny as mankind's Saviour. So close was their alliance of hearts that, all the way from the Annunciation to Good Friday, they shared a virtual identity of mission and purpose.

It reached its climax at the foot of the Cross, where Mary united the interior sufferings of her soul, pierced by the sword of sorrow, with the Passion of Jesus; thereby she mystically cooperated to the highest degree in his redeeming action. Hence her title "Co-redemptrix." It means that in a subordinate and supportive capacity Mary's merits joined with the Redeemer's in ransoming the human race from sin and damnation.

In recognition of his mother's coredemptive role, the Redeemer granted her the "Marian prerogative," thus establishing her as mediatrix of all graces. By this we understand that the mother of God mediates to the human family each and every grace; and she does so in virtue of her having mediated grace's Author to us in the first place. Furthermore, Mary's own fullness of grace signifies that she is intimately linked to the Holy Spirit; so much so that all graces coming from the Father and Son through their joint Spirit reach us through that Spirit's chosen spouse and instrument.

Just as all graces flow from the Holy Spirit through Our Lady, so do all our petitions return by that same route. And the Queen-Mother and Advocate presents these petitions, enriched by her own prayers, to Christ the King seated on his Eucharistic throne.

This trio of Marian titles—coredemptrix, mediatrix and advocate—have the deepest roots in traditional Church teaching, including numerous testimonies from popes and saints alike. One of the best-known of these testimonies came from St. Bernard:

> Let us venerate Mary with every fibre of our hearts, with our most intimate sentiments and desires, since it is God's will that we should have everything through Mary.[9]

Another influential testimony came from St. Maximilian Kolbe, who zealously promoted devotion to the Immaculate Mother of Divine Grace:

> The most blessed Virgin is the mediatrix of all graces without exception.... The life of grace depends on the degree of nearness of the soul to the Immaculate One. The nearer the soul is to her, the purer it becomes, the livelier becomes its faith and the fairer its love.... We cannot look for grace elsewhere since she is its mediatrix.[10]

So enshrined in Catholic tradition are the trio of Marian titles in question that they are at least "theologically certain"; indeed, some theologians maintain that they amount to truths of faith as taught by the Church's ordinary magisterium. It is widely and confidently expected that they will be solemnly defined by Pope John Paul II in response to *Vox Populi*, a worldwide petitionary movement embracing nearly five million laypeople endorsed by 500 bishops and nearly 50 cardinals.

The Mother of Life

Our redemption from original sin and reinstatement in supernatural life is the first and foremost grace won for us at such cost by Our Lord and his coredemptrix-mother. The New Adam and the New Eve reversed the disastrous situation brought about by the Original Sinners—our first parents. Grace now abounds where all was sin and despair. God and his mother have launched into being a brave new world of divine life destined to become eternal glory in the City of God.

God's mother is ours also: this is a key factor in the drama of redemptive grace, as Pope John Paul II sees so clearly:

> Mary's motherhood in our regard does not only consist of an affective bond. Because of her merits and intercession she contributes effectively to our spiritual birth and to the development of the life of grace within us. That is why she is called "Mother of Grace" and "Mother of Life."[11]

This simply reaffirms what a host of authorities have been saying from earliest times. Already in the second century St. Irenaeus[12] stated that whole multitudes of us are mystically born of the Virgin Mary through receiving the new life of grace. Whereas Eve through her disobedience and disbelief brought ruin upon herself and her natural descendants, Mary's obedience and belief became the "cause of salvation" for herself and the many spiritual descendants to be born of her.

Pope Paul VI referred in his *Credo* to Mary's role in conceiving and nourishing the grace-life within us:

> We believe that the New Eve, the mother of the Church, carries on in heaven her maternal role with regard to the members of the Church, cooperating in the birth and development of divine life in the souls of the redeemed.

Vatican II echoed this when it speaks of Mary as "our mother in the order of grace."[13] She mediates to us the life of her Son, and by her intercession procures the graces we need on our earthly pilgrimage. All this Mary does with a mother's love, which is all the more tender and solicitous on account of her holiness and charity. Thus St. Aelred could write:

> Through Mary we have a much better mother than through Eve from the fact that Christ was born of her. Mary is therefore more our mother than our

natural mother.[14]

Grace Is Many-Splendoured

St. Paul spoke about "the unsearchable riches of Christ" (Eph. 3:8). Here he was referring to the manifold graces made available to us by Christ the King enthroned in the Eucharist. The universal distribution of these graces is in the hands of Mary, Mother of the Eucharist. Let us now briefly survey the main forms and aspects of this many-splendoured mystery.

The drama of divine grace in the human soul begins at Baptism. This sacrament infuses into us, in the first place, the presence of the three Divine Persons indwelling us as guests. Besides this so-called uncreated grace, we receive into our being a share of the Trinitarian life; this is known as sanctifying grace, which remains in us habitually. Along with it we receive three very special powers enabling us to know, love and trust God in a supernatural way; we refer to them respectively as faith, hope and charity.

Also part of our endowment at Baptism are the cardinal virtues and the seven gifts of the Holy Spirit. All the aforementioned items comprise the equipment, so to call it, that enables us to respond to God as becomes his adopted children and future citizens of heaven.

Actual Grace

But there is a further and indispensable kind of grace needed for this complex supernatural equipment to become operative in the first place. We call it actual grace. It is a transient intervention by God needed in every single case to stir our supernatural life into action. Each time, then, that we make an act of faith, or adore the Eucharistic Lord, or invoke his mother, or forgive someone who has trespassed against us, or overcome a temptation, or do a service to our neighbour, or go to Confession, or offer God a cross He has asked us to carry, or feel moved to praise the Creator for the beauties of nature, we do so thanks to actual graces moving us thereto.

It is amazing to reflect that the millionfold actual graces each individual receives in the course of a lifetime all without exception come through Mary's mediation and intercession. Indeed, this applies to every single grace of whatever kind. So each and every grace is Marian. Each aims at making us more and more Mary-like—the sure way of achieving Christ-likeness. Each comes to us perfumed by her holy hands as the gift of a mother's love.

Graces of the Eucharist

While all graces originate from the God of grace truly present in the Blessed Sacrament, by his ordinance their channel to us is the Mother of Divine Grace. Some of the richest and choicest of these graces happen to derive directly from the sacrament itself, as we shall now see.

We begin with the Mass. To quote Pope John Paul II:

> It is the means Christ left us to take part in the sacrifice of the Cross as if we had been present.[15]

Thus the Mass makes the original Cross-sacrifice actual and accessible in the living present, pouring out upon us the torrents of grace won on Good Friday by the divine Victim and the coredemptive compassion of his mother. The propitiatory graces of the Mass serve to remit sins and their punishment. And its impetratory (that is, "asking") graces bring about the conferring of gifts both supernatural and natural. As we saw earlier, St. Ignatius was given a mystical awareness during Mass that Mary was the "portal" of the divine gifts flooding his soul.[16]

As for Holy Communion, its graces are legion. For it is the bread of life and greatly increases sanctifying grace within us. Furthermore, it signifies and deepens our unity with all fellow-members of Christ's Mystical Body.

Adoration of the Blessed Sacrament brings us into the intimacy of the tabernacle, uniting us in faith and love with the Source of grace himself. His mother co-adores with us, interceding at the same time for us to come ever closer to the God hidden in the Host.

When he coined the title *Our Lady of the Blessed Sacrament,* St. Peter Julian Eymard composed the following prayer; in it he happily links all three aspects of the Eucharistic mystery with its companion mystery of Mary's co-presence and overall superintendence of grace:

> Immaculate Virgin, mother of Jesus and our mother, we invoke you under the title of Our Lady of the Blessed Sacrament because you are the mother of the Saviour present in the Eucharist. From you He received the flesh and blood with which He feeds us in Holy Communion. We also invoke you under that title because the grace of the Eucharist comes to us through you, since you are the channel through which God's graces reach us....
>
> Teach us to pray the Mass as you did, to receive Holy Communion as you did, and to adore our Lord in the Blessed Sacrament with some of your love and devotion. You are the perfect lover of Our Lord in the Eucharist. Grant us the grace to know him better, to love him more, and to centre our lives around the Eucharist.
>
> Virgin Mary, Our Lady of the Most Holy Sacrament ... pray for us and grant to all the faithful true devotion to the Holy Eucharist, that they may become worthy to receive it daily.[17]

Grace and Sacraments

All the remaining sacraments not only originate from the divine presence in the Eucharist but are oriented towards him. Vatican II was explicit on this point:

> The other sacraments, and indeed all ecclesiastical ministries and apostolic works, are bound up with the Eucharist and oriented towards it. For in the Blessed Eucharist is contained the whole spiritual good of the Church, namely Christ himself, our Pasch.[18]

Like all graces, those proper to each sacrament bear distinctively Marian and maternal characteristics through being mediated by the Immaculate Co-redemptrix. Thus through the grace of Baptism she assists at the birth of her spiritual children into the supernatural world of God's life and love. Confirmation reinforces in our lives the influence and power of the Holy Spirit, whose chosen spouse possesses in their fullness his sevenfold gifts.

Penance is the sacrament of God's compassion and forgiveness. It is also the sacrament of fresh beginnings, of divine encouragement, and of brave resolutions for the future. Confessional grace flows abundantly into all these areas of the human spirit—wherein the Mother of Mercy and Refuge of Sinners finds rich scope for her tender love towards her children. Another aspect of this sacrament especially dear to Mary's heart is that its grace prepares us to receive her Son more worthily in Holy Communion.

As for the Sacrament of Anointing, the grace produced by it reflects the solicitude felt by Mary, Health of the Sick, towards sick and suffering humanity. The anointing with oil is essentially designed to produce peace and serenity of mind as well as a measure of physical relief. When administered to the dying, its sacramental grace is enhanced by the presence of her whose prayers we so often invoke against this very hour.

Marriage-grace holds deep significance for Mary, mirroring as it does the union between her Son and his worldwide Mystical Body, the Church. As she did at Cana, the mother of Jesus ensures for bridal couples an abundant and ongoing supply of wine—the high-quality Messianic wine of matrimonial grace—for their joint journey down the years.

Finally we come to that prince among sacraments—Holy Orders. At what might be called the operational level, the Church recognizes in Holy Orders its mainspring, its very nerve-centre. For it supplies the Church with those who in turn supply it with the sacraments of the Eucharist, Penance, Confirmation and Anointing. The mediatrix of grace cherishes her priestly sons because of their sacramental configuration to the great High Priest and their intimate involvement with the other sacraments, notably the Eucharist. This key subject is dealt with more fully in a subsequent chapter.

Mary and Charisms

Charisms, to quote Vatican II, are special graces of the Holy Spirit that render chosen faithful "fit and ready to undertake various tasks and offices for the renewal and building up of the Church."[19]

The mother of the Church clearly plays a leading role in the distribution of these exceptional graces, all of which contribute in their diverse ways to the well-being of the whole body by serving its current needs.

The charisms are granted by God primarily for the good of others rather than of the recipients. St. Paul enumerates nine of these special graces; they range from prophecy and the gift of tongues to the power of working miracles.

Prominent among charismatic phemomena in the present age are apparitions of the Virgin Mary. The privileged spouse of the Holy Spirit selects certain individuals as visionaries, to whom she makes herself visible and audible. Their role is to relay to us the heavenly messages she communicates; depending on circumstances, these are warning or encouraging, instructive or inspirational.

To take three well-known examples. Our Lady's Guadalupe apparitions mightily stirred the faith and Marian devotion of millions, besides promoting one of the most phenomenal waves of conversions in Church history. As for Lourdes, it highlighted Mary's sinlessness and fullness of grace, also reminding us how basic and indispensable is prayer. Thirdly, Fatima underlines the need our world has for penance and prayer.

Marian grace flows superabundantly in her worldwide shrines. And what this grace promotes there above all is devotion to the Eucharist. Thus Guadalupe is a stronghold of the Blessed Sacrament. Mass, Holy Communion and adoration—this Eucharistic trio is deeply structured into the Guadalupe programme.

The same applies both to Lourdes and Fatima. The mother of the Eucharist spreads her Redeemer-Son's grace into millions of pilgrim hearts, filling them with the peace and promise of eternal life.

Treasuring Grace

"If you but knew the gift of God!" (Jn. 4:10). Our Lord had his gift of grace in mind when He said this to the Samaritan woman. All of us can to varying degrees apply the Lord's words to ourselves. Only his mother has properly understood and appreciated the magnitude of the divine gift—Redemption and the grace-giving treasures it brings. Frequently, then, and fervently we should ask Mary, when we approach her Eucharistic Son's throne of grace, to win for us a richer understanding and estimation of what He offers us.

Being a share in God's own life, grace is not only precious beyond rubies but beautiful beyond compare. This explains the dazzling beauty of Mary, whose fullness of grace has now blossomed into glory. All the way from Guadalupe to modern times, visionaries testify to the glowing loveliness of God's mother. St. Catherine Labouré saw her enveloped in divine light, while grace streamed from her hands like rays upon her sinful human family. Similarly, the young Fatima seer, Francisco, described the Virgin as "all light."

Souls in a state of grace share in this heavenly loveliness and light. "Divine grace," declares St. Thomas, "makes us beautiful, as does light."[20] What this really means is that sanctifying grace effects an image of God's uncreated beauty in the soul, remoulding it to the image of the Son of God (cf. Rom. 8:29). And that image, according to St. Paul, is the reflection of God's glory and the image of his substance (cf. Heb. 1:3).

Testimony of Mystics

Numerous mystics have corroborated this from their own experiences. Names such as Saints Catherine of Siena, Mary Magdalen of Pazzi and Ignatius Loyola here come to mind. So overpowering is the beauty of a soul in a state of grace, they equivalently tell us, that we would literally die of an excess of joy were we to behold it.

St. Paul, ever a realist, puts us on our guard against losing this precious gift of grace through serious sin. For, he realizes full well, we are of ourselves weak, wayward, wilful, fickle, sin-prone. All the more reason, then, why we should cling to God for protection and strength. A well-known text runs:

> We have a treasure, then, in our keeping, but its shell is of perishable earthenware; it must be God, and not anything in ourselves, that gives it its sovereign power.[21]

In this context we get a fresh insight into what a wonderful grace the Blessed Sacrament is in itself, making Our Lord instantly accessible when we call upon him for help and strength against temptation. St. Francis of Sales observes:

> The Almighty manages our hearts so dexterously that He remedies our weakness by his divine strength, though He does not infringe our liberty.[22]

Our Lady of the Eucharist follows our spiritual progress with the keen interest and loving heart of a mother. Her overriding concern is that we remain ever in a state of grace; also, should we forfeit it through serious sin, that we return to God's friendship without delay. Mary's all-powerful intercession obtains even for hardened sinners the grace to rise again after a fall and, their human frailty notwithstanding, to persevere in God's friendship. Cardinal Newman wrote in this connection:

> Many a poor outcast who sins repents, and is with difficulty kept just within the territory of grace.[23]

---

[1] Pope John Paul II: REDEMPTOR HOMINIS, 20
[2] Vatican II: PRESBYTERORUM ORDINIS, n.5; *Lumen Gentium*, 11
[3] The Marian Movement of Priests: TO THE PRIESTS, OUR LADY'S BELOVED SONS (11th Edit. 1995): Message given on 21 August 1987, 430

---

[4] John Gerson: OPERA OMNIA, IX, 413
[5] Gerard Manley Hopkins: POEMS AND PROSE: Selected by W. H. Gardner: The Blessed Virgin Compared To the Air We Breathe (Penguin) 55–58
[6] HEB. 4:16
[7] 1 KINGS 2:16, 19–20
[8] Pope Pius IX: INEFFABILIS DEUS: the Bull proclaiming Mary's Immaculate Conception, 8 December 1854
[9] St. Bernard: SERMO DE AQUEDUCTO, 7, Opera Omnia V, 279
[10] St. Maximilian Kolbe: quoted in EPH MAR 21 (1971), 218
[11] Pope John Paul II: GENERAL AUDIENCE CATECHESIS ON 25 OCTOBER 25, 1995. (Reported in *L'Osserv. Romano*, 1 November 1995)
[12] St. Irenaeus: ADVERSUS HAERESES, 3, 16, 4; 3, 22, 4
[13] Vatican II: LUMEN GENTIUM, 61
[14] St. Aelred of Rievaux: SERMO 2 IN NATIV. PL 195, 323C
[15] Pope John Paul II: MESSAGE TO THE LOURDES EUCHARISTIC CONGRESS, 21 July 1981
[16] ST. IGNATIUS LOYOLA: PERSONAL WRITINGS. Translated with Introduction by Joseph A. Munitiz, S.J. and Philip Endean, S.J. (Penguin Classics) pp.78, 378
[17] St. Peter Julian Eymard: IN THE LIGHT OF THE MONSTRANCE: Edited by Charles DeKeyser, S.S.S., (Cleveland), 1947
[18] Vatican II: PRESBYTERORUM ORDINIS, 5
[19] Vatican II: LUMEN GENTIUM, 12
[20] St. Thomas Aquinas: COMMENTARY ON PS. 25:8
[21] 2 COR. 4:7
[22] St. Francis of Sales: TREATISE ON THE LOVE OF GOD, (London) 1884, Bk 2, ch. 12
[23] John Henry Cardinal Newman: DIFFICULTIES OF ANGLICANS, (London) 1850, 1, 249–250

CHAPTER EIGHT

Mary, Eucharist, Church

We honour Mary both as mother of the Eucharist and mother of the Church. How closely intertwined these two mysteries are is indicated by Mary's dual maternal role in their regard. And this role further indicates how intimately she is caught up into her Eucharistic Son's redemptive mission now operative in and through his Mystical Self, the Church.

That mission began when the Virgin of Nazareth, as full of faith as she was of grace, consented to become the Redeemer's mother. All the redeemed were by the same token mystically conceived in her womb; that is, from Mary were born not only Christ the Head physically but, spiritually, all members of his Mystical Body scattered across the world in the coming centuries. "In conceiving Christ," Fr. Michael O'Carroll puts it compactly, "Mary conceives Christians."[1]

The *Catholic Catechism* duly reaffirms this, recalling the age-long traditional teaching that we receive the new life of Christ thanks to our spiritual birth from the Virgin of the Annunciation. The *Catechism* text reads:

> Jesus is Mary's only Son, but her spiritual motherhood extends to all men whom indeed He came to save ... that is, the faithful in whose generation and formation she cooperates with a mother's love.[2]

Defining Moments

Thus the Annunciation, when the Virgin pronounced her joyous

Yes to God's initiative, was the first defining event in the drama of Christ and his Church. The second such event was at Cana. There Mary's mediation inaugurated her Son's messianic ministry through his transformation of water into wine. This in turn led to the transfiguration of that humble marriage-feast into a symbol, a figure, of the prospective nuptials between the Son of God and his bride, the Church.

Mary's third defining contribution to the Christ-Church drama was on Calvary. There, amid the Good Friday darkness, she witnessed the mystical birth of the Church, which emerged as the New Eve—symbolized by the blood and water—from the pierced side of the New Adam. More than that, the Mediatrix of All Graces participated in her Son's redemptive passion through her co-redemptive compassion. A short while before, Mary had received from him the commission to be spiritual mother of redeemed humanity. That is, the dying Saviour appointed her mother of the newborn Church symbolized by the blood and water that issued from his side.

The fourth defining influence exerted by Mary in the Christ-Church relationship was at Pentecost. This event was in effect the Church's official inauguration ceremony, the formal launching of Peter's Ship into the high seas of history. Again Mary made a major contribution through her trusting faith and prayer, thus becoming, as at Cana and Calvary, an indispensable instrument of the Holy Spirit.

Scripture very significantly underlines that the mother of Jesus was among those who, assembled with the apostles in the Cenacle, "continued in one mind in prayer" (Acts 1:14). Commenting on this, Vatican II intimates that it was Mary's all-powerful intercession which brought down the gift of the Spirit—the same Spirit who had never ceased to overshadow her ever since that far-off day in Nazareth.[3] Pope Pius XII echoed this teaching:

> Mary it was who by her powerful intercession obtained for the new-born Church the prodigious Pentecostal outpouring of that Spirit of the divine

Redeemer who had already been given on the cross.[4]

In a Eucharistic Perspective

These four landmark events in Mary's role as Mother of the Church are strikingly reflected in her parallel role as Mother of the Eucharist.

The Annunciation saw Mary's wonderful faith rewarded by the Incarnation. The Word came down from heaven and was made flesh in her womb. Now, in the Eucharistic mysteries, it is at the words of consecration that the same Word comes down from heaven onto our altars. And the faith of the Church, to which we owe all this, originated with the Virgin of the Annunciation, now Mother of the Eucharist. Hence, as a noted Mariologist points out, the Church's mother merits the corollary title: "Mother of the Church's Faith."[5]

The Cana episode also resonates throughout the Eucharistic mysteries. Mary's faith was instrumental in producing her Son's first-ever miracle. And this miracle, besides foreshadowing the miracle of transubstantiation, transformed the simple wedding festivities into what the Eucharist mystically represents: namely, a messianic banquet in which is celebrated the marriage between the Divine Bridegroom and his bride, the Church.

As for Calvary, its Eucharistic import is evident and massive. The Mother of the Eucharist re-lives the real-life sacrifice of her Son in every Mass that is offered; again and again she unites herself with him as co-offerer and co-offered. And in union with her so does the whole Church.

Finally, the Pentecost mystery, too, features vitally in the Eucharist. In every Mass—in the prayer known as the *Epiclesis* —the descent of the Holy Spirit is invoked by the celebrant upon the offerings. And the same Holy Spirit, besides effecting the transubstantiation of the elements, gathers into the Priest-Victim's Eucharistic body his worldwide Mystical Body as a living sacrifice of praise. All this is graphically expressed in the fourth Eucharistic Prayer:

Father, may this Holy Spirit sanctify these offerings.

> Let them become the body and blood of Jesus Christ our Lord, as we celebrate the great mystery which He left us as an everlasting covenant.... Lord, look upon this sacrifice which you have given to your Church, and by your Holy Spirit gather all who share this one bread and cup into the one Body of Christ, a living sacrifice of praise.

The Church's Offering

As we have seen, the mother of the Church participates actively in every single Mass, offering her Son and herself to the Eternal Father for the salvation of mankind. And with her the entire Church is co-offerer and co-offered along with the great High Priest and Victim.

Every Mass, in other words, has what Vatican II called "a public, social nature."[6] Pope Paul VI, after noting that this idea is "most helpful in throwing light on the Church," added some no-less-helpful observations of his own:

> When the Church, together with Christ, performs the function of priest and victim, it is the whole Church that offers the sacrifice of the Mass and the whole Church is offered in it.... Any Mass, even if celebrated by a priest in private, is itself not private; it is the act of Christ and the Church. In the sacrifice which she offers, the Church learns to offer herself as a universal sacrifice. She is also applying to the whole world, for its salvation, the redemptive virtue of the sacrifice of the cross, which is unique and infinite. Every single Mass that is celebrated is offered not just for a certain number but for the salvation of the world as well.... Every single Mass gives rise to an abundance of graces for the salvation of the priest himself as well as for the whole Church and the world at large.[7]

The Universal Mother

In saying all this we are touching upon the mystery known as the

Communion of Saints. This is really a synonym for the Church viewed in its totality as a corporate reality that is history-long and worldwide; a tripartite (consisting of three parts) immensity extending over the three zones of God's Kingdom—earth, heaven and purgatory.

St. Augustine referred to this mystical society as "the one Christ, Christ in his totality."[8] Here he was simply expanding on what St. Paul said about the Saviour: "He is the Head to which the whole Church is joined, so that the Church is his Body, the completion of him who everywhere and in all things is complete" (Eph. 1:22–23).

The Eucharist is equally sign and cause of the unity that binds together all members of the Lord's Mystical Body. And this unity achieves in every Mass its perfect expression, because Christ's far-flung members, together with Mary, are conjoined with him as offerer and offered alike. Each time, then, that "we break this bread and drink this cup," the saints in heaven and the souls in purgatory join hands and link hearts with us in worshipping the Eucharistic Lord. And we have the privilege of co-worshipping with such distinguished company because we are members of that Church which is mothered by Our Lady of the Eucharist.

The Mary-Church Relationship

Mary is God's creature; yet she is also God's mother. This is the first paradox about her. The second is that Mary is a member of the Church—indeed, its highest and holiest; yet she is at the same time the Church's mother, as well as being mother of its chief treasure and the source of all life and holiness—the Eucharist.

In discussing the Mary-Church relationship, Vatican II commented that Mary is "a type of the Church through her intact faith, her firm hope, and her genuine charity."[9]

The word "type" means in theological usage someone or something that foreshadows some prominent future person or reality. In saying that Mary is the Church's type, we mean that right from the start she is the shining model, the living embodiment, of what the Church is in her inner self—the sinless bride of Christ without stain; and, too, of what the Church will become once it has attained its final destiny in the glory of God's kingdom.

Through her assumption into heaven, the mother of God has already achieved that destiny. Accordingly she is the exemplar, the archetype, the prototype, the icon, the inspiring personification of the very perfection and consummation towards which the Church aspires. In a word, Mary has arrived, whereas the Church Militant still faithfully plods its way, day after day, on its arduous pilgrimage towards the longed-for Parousia—the return of Christ in his glory—and the paradisal world this will usher in.

Apostolic Zeal

Again seen as a type or mirror of the Church, Mary is also traditionally hailed as the New Eve, the mother of all who share her beloved Son's truth and life. From her place alongside the Eucharist, Mary constantly mother-loves each individual member of the Church-Body, bestowing on them, in the words of Pope Pius XII, "that same motherly care and fervent love with which she fostered the suckling infant Jesus in the cradle."[10]

As we have seen, the New Eve's faith is the fountainhead of our own. As for her hope and charity, they warm our cold hearts and move us to be apostolic and self-sacrificing in God's service. For the Holy Spirit has never ceased to overshadow Mary ever since that momentous day in Nazareth. And, ever since that other momentous day of the rushing wind and tongues of fire, Mary has yearned to spread her Son's kingdom throughout the world. To this end she kindles the Church's apostolic zeal in bringing the treasures of the gospel into human lives. The Holy Father has said on this subject:

> On the day of Pentecost, the Mother of the Church irradiated the power of her intercession over the Church as mother, and protected the apostolic zeal by which the Church still lives, generating for God the believers of all times and all geographical areas.[11]

Mary has therefore with good reason been termed "the star of evangelization." As Queen of the Apostles she superintends the Church's mission to souls. And as mother of the Eucharist she clearly recognizes that this sacrament is "the source and culmination of all evangelization."[12] Nor could this be otherwise, given that the Blessed Sacrament is the Lord's living presence and therefore the Church's paramount treasure.

Outreach to the World

Balthasar and several other authors have stressed the need for a fresh and vibrant missionary outreach to today's world. And the dynamic required for this evangelization, they are convinced, must be generated largely through Eucharistic adoration. The reason is that the very act of worshipping Jesus, Master of the Apostles, has a built-in apostolic dimension, kindling in hearts a deep concern for the needs, material as well as spiritual, of our fellow-humans. John Paul II has touched upon this theme:

> Evangelization through the Eucharist, in the Eucharist, and from the Eucharist—these are three inseparable aspects of how the Church lives the mystery of Christ and fulfils her mission of communicating it to all people.... In addition to the preaching of the message, the consummation of evangelization consists in the building up of the Church, which has no real existence without the sacramental life culminating in the Blessed Eucharist.[13]

The Church's zeal for souls, generated in her, through the help of Mary's prayers, on the day of Pentecost, has produced down the centuries legions of outstandingly apostolic men and women. From their ranks have come many canonized saints, those giants of the spiritual life. One and all, they drew their light and strength from the Eucharistic Saviour and his ever-present mother. From this same source they further drew a burning desire to bring the God-Man's presence into the lives of others.

Another secret underlying the zeal of the Lord's apostles in all ages is that, through Mary's intercession, they are given a deep appreciation of the unique value of each individual soul. We see this value reflected in the price paid by the Redeemer for ransoming souls from sin and eternal punishment.

"He loved me and delivered himself for me" (Gal. 2:20). Every single one of us can make St. Paul's proud claim his own. Hence the Church cherishes each individual as a pearl of great price. For this reason St. Francis of Sales could say: "All the world together is not worth one soul."[14] Cardinal Newman fully endorses this evaluation:

> The Church regards this world, and all that is in it, as a mere shadow, as dust and ashes, compared with the value of one single soul. She holds that, unless she can, in her own way, do good to souls, it is no use her doing anything.[15]

Love for the Church

One of the Marian paradoxes mentioned earlier is that Mary, though mother of the Church, is nonetheless, like ourselves, one of its members, albeit the first and holiest. This paradox can be seen mirrored in Mary's relationship to the Incarnate Word, which prompted St. Augustine to address God's mother in the words:

> He who made thee is made in thee. He is made in thee through whom you were made.... Give milk, O mother, to him who is our food; give milk to the bread that comes down from heaven.[16]

Mary teaches us and urges us to love the Church with filial ardour. For, besides being her Eucharistic Son's bride, the Church is likewise the mother who, after conceiving us through Baptism, guides, sustains and nourishes us on our pilgrimage through time to eternity.

In her manifold activities, the Church imitates and participates in Mary's motherhood over both Head and members of the Mystical Body. Moreover, Mary's intercession constantly supports the Church in everything she does. Thus she and the Church cooperate in begetting and fashioning Christians here on earth. To quote Pope John Paul II on the subject:

> Mary gave the Lord to the world, realizing in herself the type of the Church for the first time; and, by following Mary, the Church in turn continues to manifest Christ to the world and mould him in the hearts of men.[17]

Our love for our mother the Church is an expression of gratitude for everything she gives us, everything she does on our behalf. "What do you ask of the Church of God?" those seeking Baptism are asked. The reply is: "Faith." And, following this supreme gift of faith conveyed through the Church, there flows to the baptized a lifelong stream of further gifts, preeminently the sacraments.

The Communion of Saints

In a word, the Church ministers to us everything making for our sanctification and salvation. And, as the product of her manifold ministry, there arises the Communion of Saints—God's society of those called by him to be holy, and rendered so by the holy things He has provided. This mystery's inner meaning is neatly encapsulated in its original Latin form—*Communio Sanctorum*. The latter word can and does refer equally to holy persons (*sancti*) and holy things (*sancta*).

Long and impressive is the catalogue of *sancta* ministered to us by the Church. Choicest among these holy things, of course, is the Eucharist; and this is made available through that other great gift of God—the sacrament of Orders. Then there is Confession, the so-called "sacrament of fresh beginnings," which, like the other sacraments, is oriented towards the Eucharist.

As for sacramentals, which raise our minds and hearts to holy people and things, they, too, come as a gift from the Church. Sacramentals include articles such as holy water and crucifixes, rosaries and medals, scapulars and holy pictures, stations of the cross and Marian shrines.

Clearly, then, gratitude and love should define our relationship to the Church; indeed, they are the two sides of the same coin. So it is easy to see why Ignatius Loyola, following in the tradition of founders like Benedict, Dominic and Francis of Assisi, stressed the importance of "thinking with the Church," by which he meant a combination of affection and obedience on our part.

St. Teresa and Others

These qualities shine out in the lives of many a saint, never more so than was the case with Teresa of Ávila. She loved the Church dearly and deeply, its multiple human flaws and failings notwithstanding, and proudly proclaimed on her death-bed: "I die a daughter of mother Church." Her great fellow-Carmelite in Lisieux similarly cherished the Church as the holy mother who enriches our lives with such precious gifts as the Eucharistic Jesus and Mary's maternal solicitude. The Little Flower's response to the Church's generous ministry was: "In the heart of my mother the Church I will be love."[18]

Characteristic of all God's saints is that they expressed their gratitude and love for the Church in what is the most effective way possible: they prayed assiduously and fervently for its needs, its fallen-away members, its apostolic endeavours, its leaders, particularly the Supreme Pontiff.

Disloyalty and Dissent

What, we may ask, is our first obligation to the Church? St. Paul provides the answer: it is "the obedience of faith" (Rom. 1:5). Our prime duty as its members is that we should be the Church's obedient children, loyal to her every teaching and ordinance. For she has been invested by her Founder with his own divine authority; hence to hear or despise the Church's word is equivalent to hearing or despising the Word Incarnate himself (cf. Lk. 10:16). Furthermore, the Holy Spirit's special enlightenment and guidance makes the Church the "pillar of truth" (1 Tim. 3:15). Consequently she is God's mouthpiece with regard to what we believe and how we are to conduct our lives. To the Church, then, we must always, as children of Mary, give our loyal allegiance and assent. A papal encyclical made this point very emphatically:

> All Christians must deepen in themselves and each of their communities that "obedience of faith" of which Mary is the first and brightest example.[19]

But, sadly, an attitude of dissent and rebellion has become quite common nowadays among Catholics. This is a product of the liberal revolution which gained momentum in the Sixties. And it did so under the impetus of what was falsely identified as "the spirit of Vatican II." Ever since, liberal theologians, catechists, and liturgists have insidiously and systematically been undermining orthodox Catholic teaching.

Dissenting Liberals

Your hard-core liberals are dissenters who freewheel their way through revealed truths. They reject the Church's magisterium or teaching authority, setting themselves up instead as a counter-magisterium. At root they are neo-modernists; that is, there are in their view no fixed truths, no dogmatic certainties, no unchanging creeds; today's doctrines are no more than current hypotheses that will inevitably evolve into different ones as time marches on. Our efforts to promote and codify this on-going evolution of Christian doctrine gives rise to what they call "process theology." Its slogan, as a leading exponent—Charles Curran—once put it with characteristic cynicism, is "creative fidelity."

In point of fact, this attitude amounts to rank infidelity. For such people are unfaithful and disloyal to the Church's sacred authority. Moreover, like their sixteenth-century counterparts, they are in reality heretics, inasmuch as they contumaciously reject one or more credal elements of the Church's doctrine.

The Smoke of Satan

An additional factor of a most sinister kind is operative in the current assault on Catholic orthodoxy and discipline. Pope Paul referred to it as the smoke of Satan within the Church. The very intensity and extent of the opposition from within the Church to its teaching and authority strongly suggests a diabolical influence aiding and abetting operations. Another tell-tale symptom is the almost pathological hatred of certain revealed truths on the part of many critics. Nor should we wonder at this. *Odium fidei*, that is, hatred of the faith—particularly Eucharistic faith—burns and rages in Lucifer, head of the fallen angels, and he kindles it in every willing instrument he can find on earth.

Three Main Targets

What all this amounts to saying is that the Church is undergoing a crisis of faith. And the crisis happens to focus for the most part upon the very three inter-related doctrines here under consideration—the Church, Mary and the Eucharist.

To begin with the Church. While remaining within it, your out-and-out dissenters flout its divine authority and reject its teachings and directives. The Holy See is criticized for its condemnation of issues such as birth control, abortion, homosexual practices, the ordination of women. And the normative *Catechism of the Catholic Church* is widely disparaged and generally disregarded. Those Catholics who fully accept the Church's traditional teaching and authority are branded as "conservatives"—a common smear-word in the liberal lexicon.

Marian doctrine, too, is heavily targeted. The Mother of God's perpetual virginity is impugned and her role in the realm of grace and its distribution downgraded. The "liberation theology" wing of modern liberalism makes the Virgin of the Magnificat into an icon for all politico-social reformers as well as an early-day spokeswoman for feminist values.

The Eucharist Under Attack

But it is the Eucharist that forms the prime target for dissident criticism and attack. As did the sixteenth-century reformers, many begin by denying the sacrament of Orders. For, if there is no ministerial priesthood, they rightly reason, there is clearly no real presence of Christ nor any renewal of his Good Friday sacrifice. All that remains within their truncated Eucharistic system is a Communion service based on the symbolic presence of Christ in the bread and wine. Everyone present, whatever their religion, if any, is invited to receive Communion, because, after all, does not the Lord's commemorative service spell fraternity, fellowship, universal outreach?

For many readers it may well come as a shock to learn that tens of millions of our fellow-Catholics no longer believe the essential mysteries of the Eucharist. Due to the influences here under discussion, faith in our Lord's true presence and sacrifice has been severely eroded.

The following statistics reflect the situation in the United States. But things are hardly better in Europe; in certain particulars, indeed, they are even worse. In January 1992 a nationwide Gallup Poll revealed that only one Catholic in three still believes that Christ's presence in the Eucharist is real, not figurative.

These statistics were confirmed by a joint *New York Times/ CBS* poll in June 1994. Of Catholics under the age of 45, two out of three hold that the Blessed Sacrament is nothing more than "a symbolic reminder of Christ." And more than half of those who regularly attend Sunday Mass described the Eucharist's status as "strictly symbolic." These regular Mass-goers total 15 million, that is, one quarter of America's Catholic population.

Mary Destroys All Heresies

The mother of the Church grieves deeply, as we can well understand, over the present crisis that has deprived so many of her beloved sons and daughters of the true faith, especially in the Eucharist.

But we can take heart from a formula coined by Pope St. Leo

long centuries ago. Addressing the mother of God, he says: *"You alone have destroyed all heresies."* This tells us, in the first place, that any false doctrine concerning Mary's Son, or the Church He founded, or the sacraments He instituted—in a word, anything and everything to do with the God-Man and his redemptive work—is incompatible with Mary's status as the sinless Virgin Mother of God.

St. Leo's formula also tells us that Marian doctrine is the touchstone of orthodoxy. As Pope Paul VI phrased it:

> Knowledge of the true Catholic doctrine regarding the Blessed Virgin Mary will always be a key to the exact understanding of the mystery of Christ and of the Church.[20]

So the mother of God as it were embodies and sums up in herself the main themes of Christian revelation. "In a certain sense," said Vatican II on this theme, "Mary unites and mirrors in her own person the chief teachings of the faith."[21] We are reminded in this context of St. Augustine's great tribute to the Virgin of the Annunciation:

> Christ is truth; Christ is flesh: Christ-truth in the mind of Mary; Christ-flesh in the womb of Mary.[22]

Because of her intimate closeness, both physical and spiritual, to the Light of the World, his mother, besides participating in the mysteries He has revealed, is their guardian and protectress. Pope St. Pius X stated this principle very firmly: "Upon Mary, as upon a foundation, the noblest after Christ, rises the edifice of faith."[23]

From earliest times Our Lady has been invoked as the "pillar of faith." In this role she destroys heresies, undoes the power of error, and exposes the falsehood of idols. Indeed, she has traditionally been identified as that mysterious woman who, all the way from Genesis to the Book of Revelation, features prominently in salvation history, not only crushing the serpent's head but finally vanquishing the great dragon.

Nobody is more aware than the Church's mother that all the

way through history it is engaged in what Vatican II described as "a monumental struggle against the powers of darkness."[24] We must place absolute confidence in Mary, asking her, in the words of a liturgical prayer, to make us "fearless in waging the battle of faith, steadfast in holding the Church's teaching."[25]

A Saint's Prophecy

St. John Bosco frequently had prophetic dreams. One of these (he experienced it on May 30, 1862) is closely relevant to the present-day crisis of faith within the Church. The prophecy is most reassuring, because it indicates that the Church will be dramatically delivered from the present crisis. And its deliverance will come about through a twin devotion to the Blessed Sacrament and Mary, Help of Christians.

The scenario of the saint's prophetic dream was a naval battle on an immense tract of ocean. A good many vessels were drawn up to attack a large, tall flagship, which was defended by some smaller craft. Here is the saint's own account of his dream:

> In the midst of this endless sea, two solid columns a short distance apart from each other soar high into the sky. One is surmounted by a statue of the Immaculate Virgin, at whose feet a large inscription reads: "*Auxilium Christianorum*" (Help of Christians). The other column, much loftier and sturdier, supports a sacred Host of proportionate size and bears beneath it the inscription: "*Salus Credentium*" (Salvation of Believers).
>
> The captain of the flagship—the Roman Pontiff—standing at the helm, strains every muscle to steer his ship between the two columns, from the summits of which hang many anchors and strong hooks linked to chains. The entire enemy fleet closes in to intercept the flagship and sink it at all costs. They bombard it with everything they have: books, pamphlets, incendiary bombs, firearms, cannons. The battle rages more and more furiously. Again and again, beaked prows ram the flagship, but to no avail. It holds to its course, unscathed and un-

> daunted. Now and then a formidable ramming operation gashes a gaping hole in its hull; immediately, however, a breeze wafted from the two columns serves to seal the gash forthwith.
>
> Meanwhile, enemy cannons blow up; firearms and beaks fall to pieces; ships crack up and sink to the bottom. In a blind fury the enemy takes to hand-to-hand combat, cursing and blaspheming. Suddenly the pope falls, seriously wounded. He is instantly helped up but, struck a second time, dies. However, no sooner is the pope dead than another takes his place.... Breaking through all resistance, the new pope steers his ships safely between the two columns.... The enemy ships panic and disperse, colliding with and scuttling each other....
>
> Some auxiliary ships, which had gallantly fought alongside their flagship, are the first to tie up at the two columns.... Many other ships, too, head for the two columns, tie up at the swinging hooks, and ride safe and tranquil beside their flagship. A great calm now covers the sea.[26]

A Second Prophecy

Yet another prophecy relevant to our times featured in the life of St. John Bosco. When the basilica of Our Lady Help of Christians was erected in Turin, he arranged for two of her great victories to be commemorated on large metal banners positioned on its facade. On one was printed 1571—the year of the victory of Lepanto, where Christians were saved from a Turkish invasion thanks to the power of the Rosary. Into the other banner were drilled the two digits "19", and they were cryptically followed by two dots.

The only reasonable conclusion to be drawn from this is that Mary's next major victory will take place in one of the few years remaining to our 20th century.

---

[1] Michael O'Carroll, C.S.Sp.: THEOTOKOS: St. Ambrose (Michael Glazier Inc.) 1982

[2] CATECHISM OF THE CATHOLIC CHURCH: (Veritas) 1994, #501

[3] Vatican II: LUMEN GENTIUM, 59
[4] Pope Pius XII: MYSTICI CORPORIS, 110
[5] Jean Galot, S.J.: MARY IN THE GOSPEL, (Maryland) 1965, 158
[6] Vatican II: DE SACRA LITURGIA, 27
[7] Pope Paul VI: MYSTERIUM FIDEI, 31–32
[8] St. Augustine: TRACT. XXVIII IN JOANN., PL 34, 1632
[9] Vatican II: LUMEN GENTIUM, 63
[10] Pope Pius XII: loc. cit.
[11] Pope John Paul II: A CONCILIO CONSTANTINOPOLITANO 1: Letter for the Anniversary of the First Council of Constantinople and the Council of Ephesus, 25 March 1981 (CTS Do 528)
[12] Vatican II: PRESBYTERORUM ORDINIS, 5
[13] Pope John Paul II: ADDRESS AT THE INTERNATIONAL EUCHARISTIC CONGRESS, Seville, 12 June 1993 (Reported in *L'Osserv. Romano*, 23 June 1993)
[14] St. Francis of Sales: INTRODUCTION TO THE DEVOUT LIFE, (London) 1943, 217
[15] John Henry Cardinal Newman: DIFFICULTIES OF ANGLICANS, (London) 1850, 1, 239–240
[16] St. Augustine: SERMO 191, 6, PL 38, 1319 Sermo 369, 1, PL 39, 1655
[17] Pope John Paul II: MESSAGE TO THE MARIAN CONGRESS IN ZARAGOSSA, October 1979
[18] St. Thérèse of Lisieux: AUTOBIOGRAPHY OF A SAINT (London) 1960, 185–186
[19] Pope John Paul II: REDEMPTORIS MATER, 29
[20] Pope Paul VI: DISCOURSE OF 21 NOVEMBER 1964, AAS 56 (1964) 1015
[21] Vatican II: LUMEN GENTIUM, 65
[22] St. Augustine: SERMO 25, 7, PL 46, 938
[23] Pope St. Pius X: AD DIEM ILLUM: Quoted in *Papal Teachings: Our Lady*, Boston, 168–169
[24] Vatican II: GAUDIUM ET SPES, 37
[25] MASS OF MARY, HELP OF CHRISTIANS: Preface
[26] St. John Bosco: BIOGRAPHICAL MEMOIRS, VII, 107–108

John Bosco's famous prophetic dream of The Two Columns in the Sea, which referred to a great battle that would occur in the future between the Church and her enemies.

CHAPTER NINE

Mary and Eucharistic Holiness

A striking feature of the early Church was the emphasis it placed on holiness of life. St. Paul did much to set this direction; again and again he urges his readers to "put on holiness" as befits "saints" called to be such by God, and stresses that the divine will for each of us is our sanctification.[1]

This sharp focus on personal holiness among the first Christians helps to explain how "Communion of Saints" soon became a descriptive label for the Church. In its original Latin form—*Communio Sanctorum*—two complementary aspects of the Church as a mystery of holiness are subtly expressed. The first tells us that the Church is a commonwealth of holy ones (*sancti*); the second, that this commonwealth is sanctified through its possessing a common wealth of holy things (*sancta*) handed down from the Apostles. Pre-eminent among these holy things, it goes without saying, are the Eucharistic mysteries.

The Church was quite right, of course, to place the high premium it did, and still does, on holiness of life. For was not its Founder the Holy One of Israel on whom we are to pattern our lives? And did He not expressly enjoin us to be perfect, even as our heavenly Father is perfect?[2] And is not his mother and ours the sinless Mystical Rose and queen of heaven and earth?

Accordingly the Church has throughout its history preached the gospel of personal holiness. Indeed, a Vatican II document devoted an entire chapter to the subject, summarizing its message as follows:

> All Christ's faithful have an invitation, which is binding, to the pursuit of holiness and perfection in their own station of life.[3]

The Source of All Holiness

> Lord God, make us truly holy by this Eucharist, which you give us as the source of all holiness.

This liturgical prayer for the feast of St. Ignatius Loyola expresses a traditional Catholic truth: namely, the Eucharistic Saviour is the wellspring of holiness, the fountainhead of all grace and sanctification. St. Thomas, for example, states categorically that "the Eucharist is the consummation of the whole spiritual life."[4] Vatican II is just as explicit:

> The holy Eucharist contains the whole spiritual treasure of the Church, that is, Christ himself.... He who is the living bread, whose flesh, vivified by the Holy Spirit and vivifying, gives life to men.[5]

What this means in practical terms is that, for us to be loyal followers of Christ and zealous apostles of his kingdom, the grace of the Eucharist is imperative. If we are to remain ever submissive to God's will and pure in body and mind, ever truthful and honest, forgiving and compassionate, brave in carrying our crosses, generous in the service of others, persevering in prayer, kind and considerate to all comers—only the God-Man abiding Eucharistically in our midst can enable us to meet testing demands like these on our Christian discipleship.

Pope John Paul II often dwells on this theme, reminding us that the Blessed Sacrament supplies in abundant measure the all-necessary grace for us to avoid sin and reach for the stars of holiness. Here is an extract from one of his homilies:

> Only through the Eucharist is it possible to live the heroic virtues of Christianity: charity, to the point of forgiving one's enemies; love for those who make us suffer; chastity in every age and situation of life; pa-

> tience in suffering and when one is shocked by the silence of God in the tragedies of history or of one's own personal existence. You must always be Eucharistic souls in order to be authentic Christians.[6]

Mary the All-Holy

Another striking feature of the Church from earliest times onwards has been its veneration of Mary as the first and foremost of her Son's disciples, the all-time star pupil in the school of Christian holiness. Across the centuries Mary has been hailed by an unnumbered chorus of voices as God's masterpiece and the flawless, radiant image of Christlikeness. In her there flourish all the virtues and beatitudes extolled in the gospel. To Mary's proudest title—*Theotokos* (Mother of God)—the Church spontaneously added its complement: *Panhagia* (the all-holy one). On this point Cardinal Newman has said the last word. "Can we set bounds," he asks rhetorically, "to the holiness of her who is the mother of the Holiest?"[7]

Pope Paul VI once suggested that the whole mystery of Mary could profitably be approached and studied from the aspect of beauty, spiritual beauty. This recalls Pius IX's comment that, when the Archangel Gabriel appeared before God's mother-designate, he beheld a soul "more beautiful than beauty itself."[8]

As we would expect, Mary's glowing spiritual beauty has been extolled by many a mystic. For instance, the Fatima visionaries described her in terms of dazzling and lovely light. St. Bernadette of Lourdes could not find words to describe the supernatural radiance of the Immaculate Virgin. And Jelena Vasilj, on asking Our Lady of Medjugorje why she was so beautiful, received the reply:

> I am beautiful because I love. If you wish to be beautiful, you, too, must love.[9]

Mary Our Model

Mary has been given to the Church by God as a perfect model

and icon of that holiness towards which He calls us all. In Vatican II's words, "Mary shines radiantly as the exemplar of all virtues," because she has been endowed from the first moment of her conception with "the splendours of an entirely unique holiness."[10]

In addition to being our model, the mother of the Eucharist is active and instrumental in our sanctification and salvation. Like every mother, she transmits something of her own likeness to her children, restoring to us that image of Christ so deeply impressed upon herself. She leads us to his "unsearchable riches" (Eph. 3:8).

In Mary's shining personal holiness we recognize those many goals and summits towards which we disciples of her Son are duty-bound to aspire. She is the woman of faith who encourages us men and women of little faith on our pilgrimage to the Land of Vision. Her buoyant hope gives us added confidence and trust in divine providence. She fires our minds and kindles our hearts with her own burning love of God and neighbour. Her complete submission to the divine will encourages us to do likewise. Her patience under the most trying circumstances; her courage in bearing her crosses; her initiatives of charity and service towards people in need—these and all her other virtues establish our heavenly mother as the pattern and ideal of Christ-like sanctity.

Ark of the Covenant

This is one of the most significant of Mary's titles in the Litany of Loreto, and has a close bearing on her Eucharistic role. The underlying symbolism is that, in her person, she is the privileged human sanctuary chosen by the God of the New Covenant as his dwelling-place on earth. For nine months Mary was literally so; the Word was made flesh and developed his human body in her virginal womb under the action of the Holy Spirit.

Throughout her life Our Lady lived in the most intimate union with the God who had received his humanity from her. What we now refer to as the indwelling of the Blessed Trinity in souls was intimately and unbrokenly realized in Mary. As mother of the Redeemer she ever remained the chosen ark of God's redemptive covenant with mankind.

Whereas the Old Covenant ark contained two stone tablets on

which were inscribed the ten commandments, its New Covenant counterpart—the Virgin of the Annunciation— became the actual dwelling-place, at once womb and sanctuary, of the God of the commandments. And whereas the former ark had housed inanimate manna, its successor enclosed within herself for nine long months that Person who is the living bread of heaven. This made Mary in effect the first-ever tabernacle of the real presence.

Mother of the Eucharist Prefigured

Herein we see a prefigurement of Mary's role as mother of the Eucharist. For nine months she was a physical tabernacle of the Most High; subsequently she became a monstrance, displaying her Eucharistic Son to the world and radiating his graces.

A further symbolism relative to Mary's ark-status lies in the so-called *shekinah*—the luminous cloud that overshadowed the Old Testament ark as a sign of God's presence. At night it became a pillar of fire to guide the people of Israel on their journey across the desert to the Promised Land.

In the New Testament's opening scene at Nazareth, God's ark-designate was mystically overshadowed by the cloud of the Holy Spirit and the power of the Most High. That scene has found its fulfilment in the Eucharist. Mary's maternal presence presides, shekinah-like and lovingly, over the Holy of Holies—that is, the living bread, the Messianic Manna, reserved in our tabernacles. There she leads us and guides us across the desert of this life to the land where faith becomes vision.

Yet another rich symbolism lies in what the Israelites called the "throne of God's mercy"; it surmounted the original ark and was upheld by two angelic figures. In a very significant way this feature foreshadowed the future ark in her capacity as the Mother of Mercy and Refuge of Sinners. Being also Queen of the Angels, Mary is escorted not just by two of them but by the entire heavenly host; along with her they ceaselessly adore the God of the New Covenant enthroned in his Eucharistic sacrament.

Finally, God's chosen ark unceasingly urges us to observe the Covenant sealed in his blood and renewed with every beat of his Eucharistic Heart.

The Alliance of the Two Hearts

As was noted in earlier pages, the expressions "Sacred Heart" and "Immaculate Heart" stand for the inner selves—the very essence and centre, that is, the personhood—of Jesus and Mary. And the alliance of their hearts tells not just of their mutual love and affection but of their joint mission, which is to sanctify and save souls. As a papal text declares:

> It is in regard to her special role in her Son's mission that devotion to Mary's heart has prime importance, for through love of her Son and all humanity she exercises a unique instrumentality in bringing us to him.[11]

A host of spiritual authorities similarly counsel us to make Mary the guiding star of faith's adventure into the God-Man's Eucharistic mysteries. Mother Teresa, for example, has assured us that the closeness of our union with the God-Man is in direct proportion to the devotion we profess for his mother. To quote her well-known prayer:

> Mary, mother of Jesus, give us your heart, so beautiful, so pure, so immaculate, so full of love and humility, that we may be able to receive Jesus in the bread of life, love him as you love him, and serve him in the distressing guise of the poor.

Well-known, too, is the tremendous devotion of St. Maximilian Kolbe to the Immaculate Heart of Mary. He likened it to "the ladder by which we climb to the Sacred Heart of Jesus." And he stressed that, for our lives to be truly Eucharistic, they need to be lived "through Mary, with Mary, and in Mary."[12]

But few saints and mystics have spoken about the union between Christ and his mother more powerfully than did St. John Eudes, the fervent apostle of devotion to the Eucharistic Heart in and through the Heart of Mary:

> Do you not know that it is Jesus who has made the

> heart of Mary what it is, and who wished to make it a fountain of light, of consolation and of every kind of grace for all who turn to her in their need? Do you not know that, not only is Jesus dwelling continually in the heart of Mary, but that He is the heart of her heart, the soul of her soul? And so, to come to the heart of Mary is to come to Jesus; to honour the heart of Mary is to honour Jesus; and to invoke the heart of Mary is to invoke Jesus.[13]

Afraid of Holiness?

"This is the will of God, your sanctification" (1 Thess. 4:3). St. Paul could not have been more explicit. His words recall the divine injunction given in the Old Testament, "Be ye holy, as I, the Lord your God, am holy" (Lev. 19:2).

Holiness is therefore not only our vocation but our duty. God wills it, commands it; consequently it is an imperative, binding and inescapable. However, while we may accept this obligation in theory, a good many of us, alas, fail to live up to it as we should. Largely to blame is our fallen human nature; and, to make matters more difficult, we live in a fallen world and are tempted by fallen angels.

But there is a further factor underlying our weakness and failures: we are inclined to shrink back from the demands of living fully by gospel standards; consequently our response to God's invitation is often nothing above lukewarm.

However, let us take heart from the fact that even some canonized saints have had similar misgivings about their response to God's demands. A notable example was St. Claude de la Colombière, an ardent devotee of the Sacred Heart and spiritual director of St. Margaret Mary. His humble admission made in private retreat-notes almost verges on repugnance with regard to holiness; anyhow, it must surely rank among the most candid prayers ever placed on record:

> My God, I have no desire for great holiness; perhaps I even have a dread of it. But if, in your mercy, you will change me and give me courage to detach my-

> self from the world, at least let me put no obstacles in your way. You know what means to take so as to win my heart. These means are in your hands. You are the master. Holiness frightens me. But you can cure me of this false and foolish fear, and make easy what seems so difficult. You alone can do this.[14]

Four Key Areas

Yes, our Eucharistic God can and does provide the effective cure for our fears and makes easy the seemingly difficult pursuit of holiness. He does so principally through the gift of fortitude; its function is to help us overcome every difficulty and obstacle standing in the way of personal sanctification and God's better service.

In this strengthening process an important role is played by Our Lady of the Blessed Sacrament. For not only fortitude but every other gift and grace of the Holy Spirit is channelled through his chosen spouse. St. Bernardine of Siena saw this truth very clearly:

> Since Mary is the mother of the Son of God who produces the Holy Spirit, therefore all the gifts, virtues and graces of the Holy Spirit are bestowed through her hands on whom she wills, when she wills, how she wills, and as much as she wills.[15]

The above phrase "all the gifts, virtues and graces of the Holy Spirit" can be summed up in one word: holiness. Like an intricate mosaic it is a unity composed of many parts, each of which merits a special study.

But here we shall confine ourselves to four key areas of Christian holiness; they shine out in the Eucharist and Mary alike, illuminating our paths like beacons in the night. These four areas or themes, which we shall now proceed to consider, are: obedience to the will of God, charity, peace, and joy.

Obedience to God's Will

While God's will is our sanctification (1 Thess. 4:3), it is equally true to say that our sanctification lies chiefly in doing God's will. Both Old and New Testament are replete with this lesson, and we see it richly illustrated in the lives of Jesus and Mary. Gazing out at us as they do from the tabernacle, it is their ardent desire that we in turn make the divine will the guiding principle of our lives.

How, then, are we to know God's will for us? The first and principal way is in his commandments. Those who observe them faithfully are worthy to be called the God-Man's mother, sisters and brothers (cf. Mt. 12:50; Mk. 3:35). Obedience to the Church's teachings and ordinances is another imperative of Christian discipleship. To heed the Church is to heed its Founder; to despise the Church, on the other hand, is to despise him whose authority it holds (cf. Lk. 10:16). We must at all costs do whatever He himself or his Church tells us; Our Lady's counsel to this effect at Cana is a gem of wisdom and sound advice (Jn. 2:5).

Another important channel of God's will lies in the general circumstances of our lives. Divine providence decides who we are and what we are with respect to social background, natural abilities, temperament, and so on. As a wise man has said, we are not permitted to choose the framework of our destiny, ***but what we put into it is our own***.

Then there are life's everyday events and happenings. We who believe in God's loving providence learn to identify the imprint of the divine will on everything that life serves up. Whether it be a duty to perform, a joy to be savoured, a cross to carry—everything becomes, for those who have eyes to see, "the sacrament of the present moment," as it has been called.

No Ifs, No Buts

As for the crosses God asks us to carry, they are in reality priceless opportunities for deepening our union with him in the Eucharist and for meriting grace, precious divine grace, which can also be offered for the spiritual good of others. This was the lesson in Our Lady's exhortation to the Fatima seers: "Many souls go to hell because they have no one to pray and offer sacrifices for them."

Mention of those seers recalls the example of St. Bernadette of Lourdes. She had much physical suffering in later life, every tiniest particle of which she offered through God's mother for the salvation of souls. But the saint had to learn beforehand the hard lesson of accepting the divine will lovingly and unconditionally. As she herself formulated this principle: "In any physical or mental pain one must say only, 'Yes, my God, without any ifs, without any buts.'"[16]

But no one has more excelled at hearing and doing God's will than was the case with his own mother. She who brought the Word into the world now helps us to be faithful to his every word. The handmaid of the Eucharistic Lord will keep us sensitively attuned and docile to his every command. And that Eucharistic Lord, whose faithfulness to his Father's will was the driving force of his life, will sanctify us more and more as the days go by.

Charity and Holiness

"Almighty God, help us to live the example of love we celebrate in this Eucharist."[17] As in this instance, the liturgy frequently reminds us that the Eucharist is essentially the sacrament of love. And his love towards us, which burns in the Eucharistic Heart of the God-Man, is, like himself, both divine and human.

The Immaculate Heart of Mary also beats with love of us as she perpetually adores that sacred presence in the sacramental mysteries. Her role in these mysteries, as St. Catherine of Siena was shown in a vision, is that of "bearer of the fire of love."[18] So Mary constantly leads us to the warmth and consolation of the Eucharistic fire. This theme inspired Edith Sitwell's lines:

> I cry of Christ, who is the ultimate fire.
> He will burn away the cold in the heart of man.[19]

To the Eucharistic presence the text may aptly be applied: "Our God is truly a consuming fire" (Heb. 12:29). St. John

Vianney saw this very vividly; if we really understood what the Mass is, he often remarked, we would die of love, consumed like moths in those divine flames.

Clearly, then, the chief virtue to be linked with the Eucharist is charity, which involves a two-way process. That is to say, besides meaning God's love for us, it stands for our return-love towards God, a love that is to engage our entire mind, heart, soul and strength. Also, and for his sake, we are to love our neighbour as ourselves (cf. Mt. 22:39; Mk. 12:31).

Increasing Our Charity

We are now in a position to see why the principal benefit deriving from every Mass we attend, every Holy Communion we make, every moment we spend before the Blessed Sacrament, is an increase within us of what is the heart and soul of holiness: namely, charity.

Charity is the master-virtue, flowing into all other departments of holiness. As Our Lord explained, his new commandment of love is the summary and fulfilment of God's moral law, supplying motivation to every other commandment. In other words, it is basically love of our neighbour that underlies our resolution not to harm him in any way—whether the harming be through stealing, bearing false witness, envy, anger, impurity, hurting his reputation, or anything else.

St. Paul, too, highlighted the primacy of charity. He exhorts us "chosen souls, holy and beloved," to "make charity our aim." (Col. 3:12; 1 Cor. 14:1). And in a well-known passage he outlines charity's agenda—everything from being patient to hoping and enduring until the last (1 Cor. 13:4–7).

Charity of the Saints

It is in the lives of the saints that we see truly shining illustrations of charity's many facets or expressions, all of them activated by divine grace flowing from the Eucharist and distributed by Mary. For example, St. Vincent de Paul drew so copiously of God's love through Mass, Communion and adoration, that he become known as "a titan of charity." His love of God was immense; so, too, was his love for his fellow men, including not only the unlovable among them but, more difficult still, the unloving. He coined the saying: "Charity closes eyes and opens hearts." This is akin to the formula attributed to Pope John XXIII: "Every man should feel in his heart the beat of his brother's heart."

Charity produces abundant fruits, all of which thrive in the climate of the Eucharist. Prominent among them are peace and joy. Now to see something of each of these in turn.

Peace and Holiness

St. James likens peace to "the seed-ground of holiness" (Jas. 3:18). Besides being a product of charity, peace is a central element in Christian spirituality, as we see reflected in the numerous references to it in both Old and New Testament. A further reflection of its important status is seen in the frequency with which peace occurs throughout the Church's liturgy, notably to do with the Eucharist.

We shall return to this. But let us first see what peace means in itself. St. Augustine defines it as "the tranquillity of order in the human spirit";[20] by which he means that our entire selves are subjected to God's will and committed to his service. As result and reward we have peace in our conscience, and, as far as possible, peaceful relations with all others.

The supreme example of total submission to the Father's will was, of course, Our Lord. Moreover, He is not only the author and giver of peace but its literal personification: in St. Paul's words, "He himself is our peace" (Eph. 2:14). And the Word Incarnate left us his peace as a bequest, a special parting gift (cf. Jn. 14:27).

Sweet Sacrament of Peace

Small wonder, then, that peace runs almost like a refrain throughout the Mass; for example, we ask the Eucharistic Lamb of God to grant us his peace, and we exchange it with each other. Eucharistic peace is memorably expressed in the old hymn:

> Sweet sacrament of peace,
> Dear home of every heart,
> Where restless yearnings cease,
> And sorrows all depart.

Many readers will have experienced for themselves the peace, the deep and consoling peace, that seems to radiate from the Blessed Sacrament, especially when we spend time in adoration. Come to think of it, this is only to be expected. For in the presence of the Prince of Peace we are as it were in a privileged Bethlehem, that is, a "house of bread." Here, too, adoring angels herald God's peace to all who join them in worshipping the Infant wrapped in the swaddling clothes of the Eucharist. And here, too, is the ever-adoring young mother, the Queen of Peace; she never ceases to bless us, her beloved children, with the words: "Grace and peace be yours abundantly" (cf. 1 Pet. 1:2).

Joy and Holiness

Well suited to be patron saint of Christian joy would be St. John the Baptist, because while still in Elizabeth's womb he "leapt for joy" at the sound of Mary's greeting (Lk. 1:41). And on that same occasion the Lord's mother, too, recorded her joy on account of the Infant still in her womb: "My soul magnifies the Lord; my spirit has found joy in God, who is my Saviour" (Lk. 1:46–47).

From this gospel episode we can draw the obvious lesson that true Christian joy is intimately associated with Jesus and his mother. When we say the Rosary we commune with Our Lady of the Visitation. Not only do we greet her in each Hail Mary; she also greets us most lovingly, bringing us a share in her own joy.

The "blessed fruit of Mary's womb" likewise shares his joy with us through the Rosary. But it is principally through the Eucharist that He does so—as is clearly brought out in the Visitation liturgy:

> Lord, may we always recognize with joy the presence of Christ in the Eucharist we celebrate, as John the Baptist hailed the presence of our Saviour in the

womb of Mary.[21]

Very significantly the Church grants a plenary indulgence, subject to the usual conditions, if we recite the Rosary (five decades) in the presence of the Blessed Sacrament. Through the Rosary, the Visitation scenario is dramatically reproduced when we jointly honour her who is blessed among women and the Infant now Eucharistically in our midst.

What, then, is joy in itself? It has been defined as that fruit of the Holy Spirit which helps us to serve God cheerfully. Joy is a by-product of charity. At the same time it is a sign, a manifestation, of inward peace; thus a liturgical prayer requests: "Lord, give us the joy of your peace."[22]

Joy of the Saints

St. Paul repeatedly makes the point that joy is an essential part of Christian life: for example, "Rejoice in the Lord always; again I say, rejoice!" (Phil. 4:4). And the Church very distinctly recognizes that joy, far from being a luxury or some optional extra, is an essential characteristic of Christian holiness, one of its staple components.

This is illustrated in the Church's procedural rules for the canonization of saints. One of the four indispensable requirements is that candidates should have displayed an expansive joy in their life and influence, howsoever melancholy they may have been by natural temperament.

Saints Thomas More, Philip Neri, Don Bosco—numerous examples like these come to mind of habitual joy, cheerfulness and humour blending most attractively with exalted holiness of life. Such people endear themselves not only to their fellow-humans but to the Lord. "God loves joyous souls," as St. Thérèse of Lisieux is on record as saying. Her Spanish Carmelite namesake, herself a notable example of joyousness at all times, expressed that same truth with characteristic humour: "God deliver us," she said, "from long-faced saints!"

"Even when in sorrow we must live in sunshine." Newman's recommendation chimes in happily with the saying attributed to the Curé d'Ars: "In the hearts of those who love God it is forever springtime."

Prayer to the Rescue

But, God knows, there can be occasions in our lives when sadness threatens to overshadow us like massed stormclouds. It may come from a variety of causes. Anyhow, whatever its source, sadness can be relieved, if not entirely lifted, by the simple yet potent remedy prescribed by St. James: "If anyone among you is sad," he says, "let him pray" (Jas. 5:13).

Eucharistic prayer is particularly effective in banishing sadness. For there we commune personally with the true presence of the Lord who wishes his own joy to be in us (cf. Jn. 15:11). We do well also to invoke the intercession of the Lord's great precursor, now adoring him perpetually in this sacrament. We should ask him to win for us a share in the joy that filled him even while still in Elizabeth's womb.

In addition, let us frequently petition the mother of the Eucharistic Jesus and the Cause of our Joy to fill our lives with this precious gift. And let us further ask her, as we do in every Hail Mary, for the grace of a happy death—that supreme moment when, please God, we shall as faithful servants enter into the joy of the Lord (Mt. 25:21, 23).

---

[1] COL. 3:12; 1 THESS. 4:3

[2] MT. 5:48

[3] Vatican II: DE ECCLESIA, 42

[4] St. Thomas Aquinas: SUMMA THEOLOGICA, Pars 3, q.73. a.3

[5] Vatican II: PRESBYTERORUM ORDINIS, 5

[6] Pope John Paul II: HOMILY ON 19 AUGUST 1979 (Reported in *L'Osserv. Romano*, 27 August 1979)

[7] John Henry Cardinal Newman: THE GLORIES OF MARY FOR THE SAKE OF HER SON, Discourse 19

[8] Pope Pius IX: INEFFABILIS DEUS, 8 December 1954

[9] WORDS FROM HEAVEN: Medjugorje Messages, (Birmingham, Ala.) 5th Edit. 1985, p. 307

[10] Vatican II: LUMEN GENTIUM, 65, 56

[11] Pope John Paul II: ADDRESS TO SYMPOSIUM ON ALLIANCE OF TWO HEARTS, 22 September 1986

[12] St. Maximilian Kolbe: WRITINGS OF MAXIMILIAN KOLBE: A Focolare Collection (1988) 16
[13] St. John Eudes: OEUVRES COMPLÈTES, VI, 187
[14] Louis Perroy: LE PÈRE CLAUDE DE LA COLOMBIÈRE, Paris, (1923) ch. 15
[15] St. Bernardine of Siena: OPERA OMNIA, 11, 379
[16] C. C. Martindale, S.J.: ST. BERNADETTE OF LOURDES, CTS, B250, 59
[17] POST-COMMUNION PRAYER FOR 7TH SUNDAY OF THE YEAR
[18] St. Catherine of Siena: quoted by M. O'Carroll in ARTICLE "ST. CATHERINE OF SIENA," ENCYCL. "THEOTOKOS," Michael Glazier Inc. (1982)
[19] Edith Sitwell: THE CANTICLE OF THE ROSE. Collected Poems, London.
[20] St. Augustine: ENARR. IN PS. 84:8–9, PL 37, 1075
[21] POST-COMMUNION PRAYER FOR MASS OF THE VISITATION OF THE BVM, (31 May)
[22] OPENING PRAYER FOR FEAST OF ST. BLAISE (3 February)

CHAPTER TEN

Mary, Eucharist, Priesthood

When the Holy Father described the priesthood as "the nerve-centre of the Church's whole life and mission,"[1] he was affirming the key role played by priests in the drama of salvation. Priests, it could also be said, are God's key-men in the further sense that to them have been given the keys of the kingdom—the kingdom of privileged sacramental treasures, notably the Eucharist and the forgiveness of sins (cf. Mt. 16:19).

Another honour belonging to priests is that they are literally God's *elite*—those He has chosen from among men (not the other way around) to wield the sacramental keys. Clearly, therefore, given their exalted status and duties, the Lord's levites are called to be holy like their Master. And for this reason they are urged in the ordination rite to "handle holy things holily."

"The priest," Pope St. Pius X used to say, "must shine like a star in the world." Similar exhortations have been made by any number of spiritual authorities. For example, Pius XII insisted that priesthood is virtually a synonym for holiness. And Pope John XXIII declared: "The holiness of the priesthood is truly the Church's first and principal strength."[2]

The Mother of Priests

Because priests play such a commanding role in God's Eucharistic kingdom, the mother of that kingdom concerns herself very specially with their lives, their work, and their sanctification. For by sharing in her Son's priesthood they are "other Christs" and the equivalent of commissioned officers in the Church Militant.

Being mediatrix of all graces, as was explained in an earlier chapter, Mary it is who in the first place distributes to priests the grace of their vocation. Indeed, Saints Bernard and John Eudes went so far as to attribute their vocation directly to Mary's special intervention on their behalf. Padre Pio may well have had the same thought in mind when he composed the prayer which begins: "O Mary, sweet mother of priests."

Anyhow, there is certainly a "Marian dimension" to every priest's life and work. Nor is anyone more sensitively aware of this dimension than Pope John Paul II. Addressing an audience of priests in Kinshasa, he said:

> May the Virgin Mary always sustain you on the way,
> and may she introduce you more and more each day
> to intimacy with the Lord.[3]

"Intimacy with the Lord"—therein lies the heart of the matter. The Lord's mother ardently desires that her priestly sons live deeply the mystery of Emmanuel: *God is with us*. Certainly they enjoy rich scope for coming close to him through their everyday contact with divine realities, notably Eucharistic ones. Moreover, as the mother of the Eucharistic Lord knows best of all, He looks on his ordained ministers not merely as servants but as friends, close associates, confidants, intimates (cf. Jn. 15:15).

Mother of Our High Priest

The Marian dimension of the priesthood as such goes back to the moment of the Incarnation. For by her consent Mary conceived the great High Priest himself, the source of Christian priesthood. In her womb Christ's sacred humanity was anointed with the so-called "grace of union"—the hypostatic union between the Eternal Word and the human nature He assumed in order to become the God-Man. That same union invested him with his priestly office, which thereafter stamped his every activity, making his entire mission and destiny, all the way from crib to Calvary, sacrificial and redemptive.

The Messiah-Priest initiated his Eucharistic sacrifice in the upper room on Holy Thursday night, and on that same occasion ordained his first priests. The following day He offered the supreme sacrifice of his life; it is now perpetuated, re-presented on our altars each time Mass is celebrated.

Standing at the foot of the cross, Mary co-offered her own compassionate grief united with her Son's torments in atonement for the world's sins. Vatican II says of that Good Friday scene:

> There Mary stood, in keeping with the divine plan, enduring with her only-begotten Son the intensity of his sufferings, joining herself with his sacrifice in her mother's heart, and lovingly consenting to the immolation of this Victim born of her.[4]

Standing now at the foot of our altars, Mary continues to co-offer herself with her Son each time He sacramentally renews his sacrifice at the words and in the hands of his ordained ministers.

In the Person of Christ

Every priest can easily identify with the sentiments expressed in this verse:

> I look into the paten's gold
> My consecrated fingers hold,
> And mirrored in its circle see
> The other Christ I'm called to be.[5]

Besides being "another Christ," a priest has been further empowered by ordination to act "in the person" of Christ. This derives from the permanent seal or character imprinted on his soul at ordination through the laying-on of hands and consecratory words of the bishop.

Through that sacrament the ordinand's humanity is configured to that of our great High Priest. Thus, in performing their sacred functions, ordained priests actually assume the person of the Word Incarnate, having been fashioned into his living instruments to continue his saving work. Moreover, each priest assumes the person of Christ in his own individual way as befits his personality, character and needs; in addition, he is enriched with commensurate personal graces.[6]

Even the eloquent St. John Chrysostom was virtually lost for words when reflecting on the awesome dignity and powers of the priesthood. He exclaimed: "Wonderful things are these—so wonderful that they surpass wonder!"[7]

What these wonderful things clearly illustrate is that the priesthood is an incarnational mystery. For the Lord's ministerial priests mediate divine realities through human lips and hands. The words that make Emmanuel into the bread of life are pronounced by consecrated lips, and consecrated hands communicate him to his faithful. As St. Gregory of Nazianzen formulated this truth, "the priest is divinized in order that he may divinize."[8]

St. Francis of Assisi once declared that, were he to meet an angel along with a priest (even an unworthy one), he would first kiss the hand that had touched the body of Christ before saluting the angel. He went on to say: "Consider your dignity, you my brethren who are priests, and be holy, because God is holy."[9]

Identical Areas of Operation

A further reason why priests are so specially dear to the mother of the Church is that their essential mission and work coincide so closely with her own. The areas of operation, so to call them, common to both Mary and priests—the Eucharist and the general sanctification of souls—are practically co-terminous.

The Eucharistic area of operation in the respective roles of God's mother and his priests is clear. Mary's ready acceptance of God's will brought about the Incarnation of the Eternal Word in her womb, while priests, in St. Peter Julien Eymard's words, "make Jesus Christ incarnate every day through the consecrating power inherent in their priesthood."[10]

As for the general work of sanctifying souls, Mary's intercession to this end is unceasing. Priests for their part perform their task in this area mainly by administering the sacraments, preaching and instruction.

We can explain all this another way. The operations of Mary and of priests serve, each in their own mode, Christ's twofold Body—the Eucharistic and the Mystical. Mary mothered the sacred body of Christ and now perpetually adores it in the Eucharist. The priest produces that body through the words of consecration, distributes it to the faithful, and reposes it in the tabernacle for our adoration.

As for Christ's Mystical Body, the Church, Mary is its vigilant mother concerned to bring sanctification and salvation to its every member. Priests are called to share the same concern as Our Lady in serving the Church, one vital additional instrument entrusted to them being the "power of the keys" in pronouncing God's pardon on sinners in the sacrament of Confession.

Priestly Holiness

Personal holiness, it cannot be emphasized enough, is absolutely vital and central to the priesthood. Ordination invests priests with a sublime dignity and responsibilities that demand holiness of a high degree. To quote Pope St. Pius X once again, "a priest must shine like a star in the world."

Ordination also confers an ongoing supply of grace that enables priests to live up to the lofty standards set by our High Priest. St. Paul refers explicitly to this special Ordination-grace when he exhorts Timothy:

> I would remind thee to fan the flame of that special grace which God kindled in thee, when my hands were laid upon thee (2 Tim. 1:6).

The flame of priesthood is lit at the sacred fire "cast on the earth" by the Eternal Priest—the fire of faith and redeeming love. The brighter that flame rises in a priest, the more radiant a beacon does he become in the world's darkness. St. Bernard coined an axiom to this effect: "The shepherd's flame is an illumination for his flock."

Vatican II's document on the priesthood highlights the primacy of personal holiness. For example we read:

> Priests have a special obligation to acquire perfection because they were consecrated afresh to God when they were ordained.... A priest's personal holiness helps to make his own ministry more fruitful.[11]

An apostle's first conquest, to quote an old axiom, must be himself; only then does his apostolate become truly fruitful. Or as St. Charles Borromeo expressed this principle: "Sanctify a priest —and you sanctify a parish."

It was a newly-ordained priest, later destined to become a bishop and illustrious theologian, St. Gregory Nazianzen, who offered this wise counsel to all preparing for ordination:

> We must begin by purifying ourselves before purifying others. We must be instructed if we are to instruct; become light in order to illuminate; draw close to God so as to bring him close to others; be sanctified if we would sanctify others or lead them by the hand or counsel them prudently.[12]

Heart of the Priesthood

St. Francis of Sales made a private vow to spend every moment preparing to celebrate his next Mass more worthily. Also he strongly urged priests to make daily Mass a lifelong practice. From this we learn how deeply he appreciated the value of the Mass and the priesthood alike.

Daily Mass has been described by Pope John Paul II as "the pivot and heart of every priestly life."[13] For the core meaning and function of the priesthood is linked with the sacrifice of our redemption and its sacramental renewal.

"*Sacerdotem oportet offerre*." This motto ("it behoves a priest to offer sacrifices") was inscribed on the ordination card of Blessed Karl Leisner, who was secretly ordained in Dachau concentration camp in 1944. The card depicted human hands in chains but holding up a chalice, the chains symbolizing a priest's captivity in the service of Christ his Master. And as part of his service to the Lord the young German martyr offered his illness and death "for the good of others."

Daily Celebration of Mass

Mass is the most important moment of a priest's day and the centre of his life. It puts him into intimate contact with the mystery of redemption whence his priesthood derives. He is brought close to the holiness of God and so reminded that he himself is called to be holy. The conciliar document on priesthood went to the very heart of the matter:

> The celebrant of Mass is not just a symbol of Christ but actually Christ at the re-enactment of the Last Supper and the sacrifice of Calvary.[14]

That same document then earnestly recommends priests to make the daily celebration of Mass a regular practice, even if no faithful can be present, since it is the act not only of Christ but also of the Church. The revised *Code of Canon Law* makes the same recommendation (Canon 904).

Paul VI's great encyclical on the Eucharist covered all these same issues most comprehensively:

> Any Mass, even if celebrated by a priest in private, is not private; it is the act of Christ and the Church. Indeed, the Church, in the sacrifice which she offers, learns to offer herself as a universal sacrifice. She also applies to the whole world, for its salvation, the redemptive virtue of the sacrifice of the cross, which is unique and infinite. Every single Mass is offered not just for a certain number but for the salvation of the whole world as well. To priests it is our paternal recommendation that they celebrate Mass each day.[15]

Furthermore, as many papal and other texts remind us, there is nothing less than a cosmic dimension to every Mass, inasmuch as all creation—that is, the whole wide world, including everyone and everything in it—is offered along with the God-Man to the Eternal Father.

The Graces of Mass

What a feast of grace accompanies every celebration of Mass is best known by her who is grace's co-redemptrix and mediatrix. In fact, it is precisely because Mass is so grace-rich that the Church warmly recommends priests to celebrate daily. By neglecting this practice, St. Francis of Sales explained to a young priest seeking his advice, the would-be celebrant deprives of precious grace not only the Church on earth and in purgatory but himself as well, forfeiting thereby invaluable personal graces.

Regarding these personal graces gained by the officiating priest, it was another distinguished advocate of daily celebration—St. Claude de la Colombière—who treasured them like rubies, as this diary entry indicates:

> Each day in my Mass He will give me new counsels, new strength. He will teach me, encourage me. He will grant me or obtain for me, through his sacrifice, all the graces I shall ask of him.[16]

A Priest's Spiritual Life

Clearly, then, a priest's whole meaning and purpose is focused on the Eucharist in general, the Mass in particular. For he is consecrator and sacrifice-offerer of the Blessed Sacrament, besides being its distributor, custodian and privileged adorer. How accurate and apt, therefore, is the Holy Father's observation: "A priest is worth what his Eucharistic life is worth."[17]

A priest is also called to devote himself, as did the Apostles, to prayer and the ministry of preaching (Acts 6:4). As regards prayer, the kind that merits top priority in a priest's life is Eucharistic adoration. His Master ever-present in the tabernacle surely welcomes him with an especial warmth and delights in his visits.

Eucharistic adoration finds a generous expression in the devotion known as the "Holy Hour," the rich rewards of which are reflected in the lives of such outstanding priestly souls as Blessed Damien, Archbishop Fulton Sheen, St. Maximilian Kolbe, plus every single pope from St. Pius X onwards.

Another important element in priestly spirituality is frequent Confession. Many popes have urged its practice, as did Vatican II in its document on the priesthood. The reason herefor is the powerful spiritual benefit conferred through the grace of the sacrament. Significantly, the principal purpose behind Confession, we learn from St. Thomas, is to purify and prepare us to participate more worthily in the Eucharistic mysteries.[18]

What many an official Church document also warmly recommends is that priests, besides being ready and willing to hear Confessions at appropriate times, should actively encourage the faithful to resort frequently to this sacrament. We noted earlier how zealously Our Lady recommends this practice in her Medjugorje messages.

Priests and Apostolate

Mention of the faithful conveniently cues us into a further key element in a priest's spirituality, namely, zeal for the sanctification and salvation of souls. The priesthood, let us recall, is essentially a sacrament of ministry and apostolate, instituted specifically for the service of the faithful. Thus every priest could well make Fulton Sheen's motto his own: "My business is souls." As for cooperating with Christ in the salvation of souls, it has been described by St. John Eudes as "the most divine of all things divine."

The Word Incarnate resident in our tabernacles pleads with all his priests, as he did with his first apostles, to lift up their eyes and see the soul-fields white for the harvest (cf. Jn. 4:35). The Queen of Apostles, who also bears the title Star of Evangelization, shares her Son's vision; more than that, she supports with her prayers every apostolic endeavour on the part of priests.

Apostolic endeavours as such flow from the Holy Spirit's promptings, and his individual gifts underlie and direct each priest's apostolic ministry. How effectively in this respect Our Lady acts for priests both as example and inspiration was highlighted by Vatican II:

> Priests find a model of docility to the Holy Spirit in

> the Blessed Virgin Mary. Led by the Holy Spirit, she devoted herself entirely to the mystery of man's redemption.[19]

While still Archbishop of Milan, the future Paul VI once said in an address to his flock: "You have immortal souls, and we priests have precious treasures to give them." This message deserves to be engraved in letters of gold on the heart of every priest.

A Priest's Faith

A striking feature of Our Lady's Medjugorje lessons is the importance she attaches to faith. She is even on record as saying there that her favourite prayer is the Creed. And, very significantly, when asked by a visionary what she particularly wanted of the local priests, she replied: "They must persevere in the faith and protect the faith of the people."[20]

As we know, our Catholic faith attains its highest and holiest summit in the Eucharist—the sacrament of faith *par excellence*. And it is here in particular that a priest's faith needs to be strong, pure and ardent. What his faith likewise needs is a good, sound grasp of the Church's teaching. To every priest applies the counsel given to Timothy by St. Paul:

> Reading, preaching, instruction—let these be thy constant care.... Two things claim thy attention: thyself and the teaching of the faith; spend thy care on them; so wilt thou and those who listen to thee achieve salvation (1 Tim. 4:13, 15).

Also required of a priest is a close fidelity and deep loyalty to the Church's magisterium, that is, her teaching authority. In the contemporary Church there is much doctrinal confusion, not least over Eucharistic truths such as the true presence and the sacrificial nature of the Mass. Causing and spreading this confusion are dissenting theologians and catechists; unfortunately their influence is strong in many seminaries as well as Catholic theological faculties.

What the mother of the Church urgently requests of today's priests is that they practise what St. Ignatius so strongly advocates in his *Spiritual Exercises*: he calls it "thinking with the Church." This makes good sense as well as sound theology. For the Church is God's mouthpiece on earth; it has the words of eternal life. Thus he who hears the Church hears the God-Man who founded it.

Today's Crisis of Faith

It is a sad irony that Vatican II, which John XXIII and Paul VI in turn had hoped would signal a new golden age for the Church, marked instead the rise of widespread dissent against the Church's teaching and authority, with the resultant decline of discipline as well as devotion. But of all post-Conciliar phenomena the most tragic and damaging has doubtless been the defection of tens of thousands of priests as well as nuns. This loss has equivalently been a severe haemorrhage in Christ's Mystical Body, the weakening and demoralizing effects of which are untold.

Going hand-in-hand with this is the crisis of faith so widespread today. Reliable opinion polls indicate that, on both sides of the Atlantic, Mass attendances have dropped alarmingly, while the belief of two Catholics out of every three now approximates more to Lutheran and Calvinist symbolism than to the traditional doctrine of Christ's real presence.

Moreover, a spirit of revolt against the Church's authority is growing. One particular organization, Call to Action, which also goes under the name We Are Church, is openly demanding that the Church give its approval to things like abortion, homosexual acts, birth control, married clergy, the ordination of women, and election of bishops by the laity. Sadly, quite a few priests (plus a number of bishops) belong to these and other rebel groups.

Vessels of Clay

St. Paul's warning words apply to priests as much as to laity: we carry the treasures of heaven in that frail and all-too-brittle earthenware which is our fallen humanity (cf. 2 Cor. 4:7). Though priests stand to benefit additionally throughout their lives by the ongoing sacramental grace of Orders, they remain vessels of clay, in constant need therefore of a strong spiritual life to safeguard their spiritual treasures and to keep themselves faithful and zealous in the Lord's service. As for the Lord's mother, she acts very specially as protectress and guardian of her priestly sons, notably in respect of their prayer life and celibacy.[21]

Many popes, saints and spiritual writers down the centuries concur in saying that serious lapses on the part of priests are invariably attributable in the last resort to their neglect of prayer. For prayer is the lifeline supplying the grace that gives fidelity and fortitude in God's service.

Many of the priestly lapses in question are against celibacy, that is, the voluntary renunciation of conjugal life for the sake of God's eternal kingdom. St. Paul's advocacy of celibacy remains as reasonable and relevant as ever: a priest is thereby more free to serve God than would be the case if he had the additional duties and responsibilities of a husband and head of a family (cf. 1 Cor. 7:32, 33).

But celibacy's chief motivation is to be found in the phrase occurring a few lines above: "for the sake of God's eternal kingdom." The Lord's priestly servants look ahead, as He bids them, to the heavenly world to come. Here on earth we have no abiding city; our true home, our everlasting destiny, lies in the City of God.

In fact, the chief motivation of a priest's life and lifework should be that eternal world to come. For there the Divine Bridegroom will celebrate the spiritual nuptials with his bride, the Church. Meanwhile, priests are the Bridegroom's chosen friends; in the Cana of this world they are stewards at the marriage-feast where the wine of grace flows abundantly. Thus they are preparing human souls to enter that happiest and most enduring of marriage-feasts in the glorious world ahead.

Through being celibate, priests increase their availability for ministry and apostolate. They are wise to heed closely the counsel given to their Cana prototypes by her whose initiative and intervention gave rise to the whole episode in the first place: "Do whatever he tells you" (Jn. 2:5).

Prayer for Priests

A striking feature of many Marian apparitions is the top priority given in her messages by the Mother of God to prayer for priests. This particularly applies to La Salette, Fatima, Garabandal and Medjugorje.

The reason is that the mother of the Church is profoundly conscious of the all-important role priests play in her Son's saving work. She appreciates how true are the words spoken by Pope John XXIII during a Holy Hour in St. Peter's basilica: "The sanctity of the priesthood is truly the first and principal strength of the Church."[22]

For priests to remain loyal to the Church's teaching authority and preach the Catholic faith in its entirety—this is a much-needed petition recommended to our prayers. Another deserving petition is that priests be burning and shining lights, men of prayer, zealous apostles, charitable towards everyone, chaste and humble at all times.

Of course, throughout the Church's history there has been this awareness that priests, because of their indispensable role, need the support of our prayers. Indeed, contemplative orders such as the Carmelites and Poor Clares make that one of their top-priority intentions. Also, many victim-souls have been inspired to offer their sufferings on behalf of priests; one thinks of two in modern times—Alexandrina da Costa and Teresa Neumann.

St. Margaret Mary was urged by Our Lord to pray incessantly for the Church's priests. Indeed, He once told her sadly that the thorns entwined around his Sacred Heart represent what He suffers from the neglect, abandonment and sinfulness on the part of priests and religious.

A novel initiative was taken by Our Lady in inspiring Christina Gallagher to set up a special centre of prayer for priests. Situated on the west coast of Ireland, Our Lady Queen of Peace House of Prayer, as it is titled, has been the source of untold blessings for priests ever since it was officially dedicated by Archbishop Joseph Cassidy of Tuam in July 1993.

The Marian Movement of Priests

Another novel initiative on Our Lady's part was the formation of this movement to help priests spiritually and to encourage laypeople to pray earnestly for them. It started in 1972 when an Italian diocesan priest, Fr. Stefano Gobbi, on pilgrimage at the time in Fatima, was praying in the little Chapel of the Apparitions for some priests whose vocations were under great strain. Fr. Gobbi received a very special grace from the Mother of God, as we read in the official narrative:

> An interior force drove Fr. Gobbi to have confidence in Our Lady's love. She, making use of him as a humble and poor instrument, would gather together all those priests willing to accept the invitation to consecrate themselves to her Immaculate Heart, to be closely united with the Pope and the Church, and to lead the faithful into the sure refuge of her motherly heart.
>
> In this way there would be formed a powerful army of priests spread across every part of the world and gathered together, not by any human propaganda, but by the supernatural power which springs from silence, prayer, suffering, and constant fidelity to one's duties.[23]

Our Lady has proved to be as good as her word. The Marian Movement of Priests, as it came to be known, is spreading at a phenomenal rate; already it numbers some 100,000 priests and 500 prelates (including several cardinals) all over the world. In addition, it musters several million laypeople affiliated to the Movement and committed to a life of consecration to Mary's heart and of prayer for priests.

The regular interior locutions which Fr. Gobbi receives from Our Lady are gathered together into a volume, the circulation of which is very large. These locutions are mainly directed at helping priests to live their consecration to the Immaculate Heart of Mary.

It is this common consecration that binds the worldwide members of the Marian Movement of Priests into a brotherhood that is close and strong without being juridically institutionalized. The Movement benefits the spiritual lives of priests enormously and deepens their love and loyalty towards the Church and the Holy See.

No wonder, then, that our present Holy Father has given his warmest blessing to Mary's priestly army so ardently dedicated to serving the Eucharistic Saviour under the banner of her Immaculate Heart.

Women and Priesthood

Pope Paul VI said on this subject:

> Mary is, after Christ and by virtue of Christ, at the summit of the organization of salvation. She precedes and surpasses the priesthood. She is in a position of superior excellence and higher efficacy.[24]

The queen of heaven, by reason of her unique privileges, transcends all other creatures, both angelic and human, in terms of holiness, privileges and power. Yet she was not given the rank of an apostle; nor did she receive priestly ordination.

The same holds for all women. This does not imply that they are of lesser dignity than men. Still less does it imply that they are discriminated against. It simply means that God's plan for his Church from the beginning has been to limit the ministerial priesthood to the male sex. This is amply reflected in Scriptural examples and throughout the Church's long tradition; also we see the practice paralleled in the Oriental Churches.

A Papal Ruling

The proponents of feminist theology have during the past few decades been campaigning vigorously for the admission of women to priestly ordination, despite some clear signals from the Holy

See that they have no case at all. But, undeterred, the feminist lobby continued to petition and pressurize the Holy See. Finally Pope John Paul II issued an Apostolic Letter outlining the Church's definitive position in the matter; it concluded:

> Wherefore, in order that all doubt may be removed regarding a matter of great importance, a matter which pertains to the Church's divine constitution itself, in virtue of my ministry of confirming the brethren (cf. Lk. 22:32), I declare that the Church has no authority whatsoever to confer priestly ordination on women, and that this judgment is to be definitively held by all the Church's faithful.[25]

The Holy Father recalled in the same document how the Church has always defended the dignity of women, holding in special honour those countless martyrs, virgins and mothers of families who, emulating Mary in their respective ways, have in every age shared in the Church's apostolic mission.

In so doing, these women were exercising their common priesthood—the priesthood of the faithful—through the faith, hope and charity received along with divine grace at Baptism. This priestly status is called royal because it shares in the unique priesthood of Christ the King as well as in his mission (cf. 1 Pet. 2:9).

---

[1] Pope John Paul II: HOLY THURSDAY EXHORTATION, 4 April 1996
[2] Pope John XXIII: HOLY HOUR ADDRESS IN ST. PETER'S BASILICA. Reported in *The Southern Cross*, 17 June 1959
[3] Pope John Paul II: A PRIEST FOREVER, Papal Texts, 106
[4] Vatican II: LUMEN GENTIUM, 8, 61
[5] Adrienne Gascoigne: THE PRIEST: in *Messenger of the Sacred Heart* (London) May 1959
[6] Vatican II: cf. PRESBYTERORUMN ORDINIS, 12
[7] St. John Chrysostom: DE SACERDOTIO, Bk 3, 4 PG 48, 6421
[8] St. Gregory of Nazianzen: ORATIO 2, 73 PG 35, 481
[9] Nesta de Robeck: quoted in THE LIFE OF ST. FRANCIS OF ASSISI (Casa Editrice Francescana) 1975
[10] St. Peter Julian Eymard: TWENTY-FIFTH DAY. In the Light of the Monstrance, Edited by Charles deKeyser, S.S.S., (Cleveland) 1947
[11] Vatican II: PRESBYTERORUM ORDINIS, 12

[12] St. Gregory of Nazianzen, loc. cit.
[13] Pope John Paul II: GENERAL AUDIENCE ADDRESS, 30 October 1996 (Reported in *The Wanderer*, 5 December 1996)
[14] Vatican II: PRESBYTERORUM ORDINIS, 5
[15] Pope Paul VI: MYSTERIUM FIDEI, AAS (37) 1965, 761–762
[16] Agnes Blundell: CLAUDE DE LA COLOMBIÈRE (London) 1963, 19
[17] J. P. Flannery, O.P.: quoted in VATICAN II, 2, 346
[18] St. Thomas Aquinas: cf. SUMMA CONTRA GENTILES, 4, 74, 7
[19] Vatican II: LUMEN GENTIUM, 18
[20] WORDS FROM HEAVEN: Medjugorje Messages (Birmingham, Ala.) 5th Edit. (1985) 59
[21] Vatican II: cf. PRESBYTERORUM ORDINIS, 18
[22] Pope John XXIII: Reported in THE SOUTHERN CROSS, 17 June 1959
[23] The Marian Movement of Priests: Introduction: TO THE PRIESTS, OUR LADY'S BELOVED SONS (11th Edit.) 1995
[24] Pope Paul VI: ADDRESS TO AN ANGLICAN GROUP (quoted in *The Catholic Herald*, 16 October 1964)
[25] Pope John Paul II: ORDINATIO SACERDOTALIS, 4

CHAPTER ELEVEN

Mary's Eucharistic Shrines

All Marian shrines soon develop into strongholds of the Eucharist. Be it Guadalupe, Lourdes, Knock, Fatima, Medjugorje, Betania, or whichever pilgrim-centre you care to mention, any site graced by Mary's apparitions grows before long into a busy sanctuary of the Blessed Sacrament.

Nor could this be otherwise. For a pilgrimage to any shrine, Marian or otherwise, is essentially a pilgrimage of faith. Now what is the highest possible object upon which faith can focus? The answer, of course, is: faith's Giver and Goal himself. And where is He to be found in person if not in the Blessed Sacrament? Therefore, Marian sanctuaries are of their very nature programmed to take on a Eucharistic dimension; in them, as our Holy Father has noted:

> The piety of the Christian people has always very rightly sensed a profound link between devotion to the Blessed Virgin and worship of the Eucharist.... In the pastoral practice of the Marian shrines, Mary guides the faithful to the Eucharist.[1]

The Holy Father has also noted a further function of Marian shrines: they serve to remind us that the Blessed Virgin is *herself* God's first and principal shrine.[2] For as Ark of the Covenant she bore in heart and womb not just the tablets of the law but the Lawgiver himself; nor just the jar with manna but the living bread which came down from heaven (cf. Jn. 6:32–33).

Finding the Two Hearts

Another way of stating all this is that every Catholic devotion, when stripped down to its bare elements, is directly or indirectly aimed at finding the Child with Mary his mother (cf. Lk. 2:12). These two are inseparable; the two hearts are intimately allied. This explains why Our Lord, as Lucia of Fatima was instructed to tell us, wishes his own Eucharistic Heart and that of his mother to be placed alongside each other and jointly honoured.

In this way it comes about that we meet the alliance of hearts in all Marian sanctuaries. There, along with God's mother, we offer our homage and adoration to him who was the fruit of her shining faith as much as of her womb. For she is called blessed because she believed (Lk. 1:45). And now in turn Mary helps pilgrims to believe ever more strongly—especially in the sacrament of her Son's loving presence and sacrifice. The Fathers of Vatican II said on this subject:

> Mary featured prominently in the history of salvation.... Hence when she is preached and venerated she summons the faithful to her Son and his sacrifice, and to love for the Father.[3]

Why Pilgrimages?

What, we may ask, is the bottom line of all pilgrimages as such? The reply is: they mirror the fact that we human beings are already pilgrims in a most fundamental sense: that is, our entire life, from birth to death, is in reality a pilgrimage through this time-world to the eternal kingdom of God. Scripture likens us to "pilgrims and strangers" here on earth (cf. Heb. 11:13). To everyone without exception this applies, because God wishes *all* men to be saved and thus attain their destiny in eternal life (cf. 1 Tim. 2:4).

It is to the queen of that heavenly world that Marian pilgrimages are primarily directed. They serve to reassure us that she is a loving mother, all-merciful, full of grace, most solicitous about our temporal needs and desires—but concerned, above all, that our life-pilgrimage should reach the shrine of eternal life safely and securely.

Now this life-pilgrimage of ours is essentially a journey of faith. For not only do the just live by faith but must make their pilgrim-way to eternal life with its help and guidance (cf. Heb. 10:38). This applies to faith understood both as a virtue and a creed; that is to say, *how* we believe and *what* we believe.

The Need for Mary

But alas, as the mother of God knows full well, there is currently a crisis of faith in wide areas of the Church, with a resultant decline in sacramental and devotional life. Central dogmatic truths, including the Eucharist and Mary's privileges, are under heavy attack. In many parishes, Confession has been marginalized almost to the point of extinction. Understandably, therefore, a good many of the faithful feel bewildered and helpless amid the confusion.

Small wonder, then, that the mother of the Church is playing a prominent role this day and age through her apparitions and messages. Besides fortifying our faith, these are further aimed at supplementing the often inadequate diet of instruction and devotion currently being served up through the normal channels to large segments of the faithful.

On the subject of Marian devotion, Cardinal Martini has warned theologians and pastors, some of whom tend to rationalize and virtually dehumanize theology into a set of dry abstractions, not to overlook "the spiritual yearnings of the Christian people." He goes on:

> Otherwise we may face a dangerous loss of warmth and feeling in our faith, our prayer and our life.... We have arrived at a point where this cold scientific attitude no longer responds to an obvious need for an attachment to Mary.[4]

The Graces of Pilgrimage

These are legion. You have only to read about shrines like Guadalupe, Lourdes, Fatima and Medjugorje to appreciate the profound spiritual fruit they produce in millions of pilgrims.

The mother of God lays great stress on interior conversion as a pilgrim's principal objective. That is, purification of conscience and a sincere purpose of amendment are indispensable for the graces of pilgrimage to flow. That is why the sacrament of Confession plays a major role in all Marian shrines. Indeed, Medjugorje has been called "the world's confessional" by reason of the huge numbers of pilgrims receiving this sacrament.

Now the underlying purpose of Confession, let us recall, is to prepare penitents to receive the Eucharist more worthily.[5] For this reason the mother of the Saviour has recommended at Medjugorje that every member of the Church should confess their sins at least once a month. And this is an integral part of her Eucharistic agenda, so to call it.

Another feature of Marian apparitions lies in the messages conveyed by Our Lady through her visionaries. Herein we see a novel verification of something said by an ancient writer: "Since Mary is mother of the Word, she has words in abundance."[6]

Meeting Our Mother

The underlying point about Marian shrines is that the Queen of Prophets, the mother of the Word, presides in them *as our mother*. And, in keeping with her maternal role, through her messages she by turns encourages, teaches, pleads, warns, guides us her children, offering us hope and strengthening our faith. Newman said of Our Lady's prophetic role:

> God's mother is the first of the prophets, for of her the Word came bodily; she is the sole oracle of truth, for the Way, the Truth and the Life vouchsafed to be her Son; she is the one mould of Divine Wisdom, and in that mould it was indelibly set.[7]

Mary also visits her shrines as the Queen of Apostles. Sr. Briege McKenna noted of Medjugorje: "People go there as pilgrims and go away as apostles." In other words, they now feel fired to share the good news with others. Similarly all Marian shrines become in their various ways centres of evangelization. An all-time record in this respect was surely Guadalupe. Once the miraculous image on Juan Diego's cloak became public knowledge, a tidal wave of conversions took place among the Aztecs.

Selecting Shrines

Each Marian shrine has its distinctive ethos, charism and human appeal—and each merits individual consideration. But we must limit ourselves here to a selection, indicating in each case how Mary transforms them into powerhouses of the Eucharist.

Of these selected shrines, all but two—Garabandal and Medjugorje—have received the Church's official approval. This does not imply, however, that the pair in question have been *disapproved* by the Church. Rather, it simply means that the respective hierarchical authorities have not yet reached an affirmative conclusion as to the supernatural character of the events and messages. Pending that conclusion, only private pilgrimages (not public ones) may be conducted there. It is helpful to recall in this context that it took the Church some 13 years to give its final approval to Fatima.

Meanwhile we are free under Canon Law to write, speak, and preach about the events and messages associated with Garabandal and Medjugorje, provided we do not in the process breach Catholic faith or morals. A further proviso is that we be fully prepared to abide by whatever decision the Church finally makes in the matter.

Guadalupe

This Marian shrine in Mexico City dates back to December 12, 1531. On that day a peasant named Juan Diego (now Blessed) saw before him, on the rugged slopes of Tepeyac hill, the Virgin Mary bathed in supernatural radiance. "I ardently desire," she said, "that a church be built here." Right from the start, then, God's mother indicated the Eucharistic orientation of her mission. Very significantly, too, Juan Diego was at the time making his way to Mass.

The rest of the story is well known. The local bishop was finally convinced of its authenticity through the sign he received and the image of Mary (she was clothed like an Aztec royal virgin in an advanced stage of pregnancy) that was miraculously imprinted on the peasant's tilma or cloak.

Once this prodigy became known, it proved to be heaven's instrument for one of the most astounding mass conversions in Church history. Some eight million Aztecs were baptized within a matter of no more than 10 years. In the wake of these conversions, hundreds of churches were built; thus the Eucharistic kingdom of Mary's Son attained ever wider horizons.

Guadalupe itself is now a world-famous shrine visited by some 20 million pilgrims a year. The miraculous image, displayed above the high altar of the basilica, appears to look down adoringly on the tabernacled Lord below. The adjoining Adoration Chapel attracts large numbers, including many adorers making the Holy Hour. Holy Communion is distributed every 15 minutes.

One of Guadalupe's most amazing and providential features concerns the Mass. In the very locality where the barbaric sacrifice of countless human victims, including babies, used to take place to appease cruel pagan deities, the holy Sacrifice of Mary's Son is multiplied a thousandfold, thanks to the numerous priests who go there on pilgrimage.

What might be called the shrine's travelling extension is the so-called Missionary Image of Our Lady of Guadalupe. It is a replica of the original, and ever since 1991 is being taken around the world for public veneration; so far 1,000 parishes have accommodated it. The public veneration of the image gives rise to a full Eucharistic programme—Mass, Holy Communions, adoration of the Blessed Sacrament. Thus the grace of the Lord's sacramental presence reaches far and wide. One of the main graces is that the same Lord as is "present" in the womb of the imaged Virgin of Guadalupe extends a powerfully protective blessing over unborn infants menaced by the evil of abortion.

Lourdes

Set amid enchanting scenery near the French Pyrenees, this is surely the best-known of all Mary's shrines and ranks among the most frequented. Here it was that in 1858 the Mother of God appeared 18 times to a 14-year-old peasant girl—Bernadette Soubirous (now Saint). Our Lady identified herself as the Immaculate Conception, thus endorsing the dogma defined by Pius IX four years previously. Her message was prayer and penance for sin. She caused a miraculous spring of water to flow; ever since it has featured in numerous cures and healings.

As she had done at Guadalupe, Our Lady of Lourdes early on gave instructions that she wanted a church to be erected. Hereby she again manifested her Eucharist-oriented purpose and plan, whereby in this theatre of Marian devotion her sacramental Son would always hold centre-stage.

Hence Jean Guitton could comment:

> Nowhere is the relation of Mary to the Blessed Eucharist so clearly grasped as at Lourdes. When a priest says Mass there, especially if he has the privilege of saying Mass at the Grotto, he knows that Mary is there, as she was on Calvary, offering her Son.[8]

Masses, Holy Communions, Holy Hours, not to forget Confessions—these reach impressive figures. An unforgettable feature of Lourdes is the candlelight procession of the Blessed Sacrament as it winds along to the strains of *Ave*, the perennial Marian invocation. Another Lourdes feature is the blessing of the sick with the sacred Host; this, besides shedding the Saviour's peace over those pathetic rows of sufferers, has been the occasion of some sensational miracles of healing.

Lourdes is jointly the City of Mary and the City of the God-Man in his sacramental mysteries. Pope St. Pius X summed up the shrine's dual status perfectly when he wrote:

> The unique glory of Lourdes lies in the fact that pilgrims from all over are drawn there by Mary to the adoration of Jesus Christ in his august sacrament; so this sanctuary seems to surpass all others in the Catholic world both as the centre of Marian devotion

and as the throne of the Eucharistic mystery.[9]

Knock

This small village in County Mayo was singled out by the Mother of God to be Ireland's future National Shrine when she appeared there one wet and windswept evening in 1879. Between 15 and 20 people of varying ages saw her; she was accompanied by St. Joseph and St. John the Evangelist. These three figures resembled statues in a group or tableau, brilliantly illuminated and set against an outside wall of the church; they remained there for nearly two hours. But the centrepiece of this tableau was the sacrificial lamb; it stood on an altar surmounted by a luminous cross. Hovering around the altar were a number of angels.

The figures appeared to move, and St. John the Evangelist, who was holding a book, seemed to be speaking. Not a word was heard, though, either from him or Our Lady or St. Joseph. Indeed, their complete silence has given rise to intense speculation ever since as to Knock's meaning and message.

The common view is that the silence was intended to reflect the silence and reverence due to the Eucharistic mysteries. But Knock's core message is surely to be discerned in the components of the flood-lit tableau set against the church wall.

First and foremost among these components is the lamb. It symbolizes the Lamb of God mystically re-immolated each time the Mass is celebrated. Standing alongside the altar is the Mother of Sorrows, who is co-offered and co-offerer every time her Son sacramentally renews his Good Friday sacrifice. The Queen of Ireland, as Mary is titled in the new basilica, has in her gift of Knock rewarded the Irish people for their heroic loyalty to the Mass during the brutal persecution of penal times.

Another component in the tableau is fittingly St. John. For in his gospel and prophetic writings the Lamb of God is a common theme; in fact, the phrase occurs some 27 times in the Book of Apocalypse. Let us recall, too, that St. John's discipleship dated from the time his great namesake—John the Baptist—pointed out to him and his companions the Lamb of God among the throngs at the Jordan.

But what was undoubtedly intended to be the tableau's centrepiece is the lamb. It symbolizes the sacrificial Lamb of God who by his death and resurrection takes away the sins of the world. And, too, it foreshadows the Masses that would be celebrated here in their tens of thousands during the years to come. Similarly foreshadowed by the lamb are the countless Holy Communions and the many hours of adoration by pilgrims coming from Ireland and abroad.

Though the Knock apparition has never been formally approved by Church authorities, it has received four papal sanctions, including the pilgrimage there of Pope John Paul II for the centenary in 1979. He was deeply impressed by the love and devotion shown to the mother of God as well as the fervour surrounding her Son in the Eucharist.

Fatima

The feast of Our Lady of the Blessed Sacrament was originally set by St. Peter Julian Eymard for May 8 but was transferred to May 13. That happened to be the very day in 1917 that Our Lady appeared for the first time at Fatima. We are surely meant to see in this happy conjunction of dates a providential pointer to the intimate link between Marian and Eucharistic devotion. That apparition on May 13 was the first of six; they culminated in the spectacular miracle of the sun, witnessed by some 70,000 people, on October 13 of that same year.

Our Lady's Fatima message emphasized prayer (especially the Rosary), penance, devotion to her Immaculate Heart, intercession for the dying and those in danger of eternal damnation; also a greater devotion to the Eucharist, including adoration and reparation for the widespread neglect and offences suffered by the Eucharistic Saviour.

Mary's message at Fatima is stark and stern. It is a clarion call to prayer, conversion, penance and sacrifices. If the message is heeded, the Virgin made clear, there would be peace and Russia would be converted; otherwise there would be a large-scale apostasy from the Church and disastrous consequences visited as punishment upon sinful humanity. Karl Rahner's warning remains as relevant today as it was in 1974: "The Fatima message is imperative, obligatory, and in more urgent need of fulfilment than ever."[10]

In 1916 (the year preceding Our Lady's apparitions) an angel calling himself the Angel of Portugal had appeared three times to prepare the children for the coming of God's mother. At his final visit he held in his left hand a chalice, and in his right a Host, from which drops of blood were falling into the chalice positioned below it. Leaving the Host and chalice suspended in mid-air, the angel prostrated himself on the ground and said the following prayer three times:

> Most holy Trinity, I adore you profoundly. I offer you the most precious body, blood, soul and divinity of Our Lord Jesus Christ, present in all the tabernacles of the world, in reparation for all the outrages, sacrileges and indifference by which He is offended.

In her first apparition Mary urged the seers to fall on their knees and say:

> O most holy Trinity, I adore you. My God, my God, I love you in the most Blessed Sacrament.

Mary also requested that a chapel of adoration be erected at the place of apparition. She stressed this devotion as an ideal way of making reparation towards the Eucharistic Lord. All three visionaries displayed great generosity in this respect, none more so than nine-year-old Francisco, who would spend hours on end adoring the "Hidden God," as he termed the sacramental Christ within the tabernacle.

Garabandal

This humble and remote mountain-village in northern Spain was between 1961 and 1965 the scene of a great number of Marian apparitions to four little girls aged between ten and eleven. In Our

Lady's two official messages as well as the numerous private ones communicated to the seers, the Eucharist was a predominant theme. She encouraged us to pay frequent visits to the Blessed Sacrament and lamented that it was receiving "less and less importance."

When the ecclesiastical authorities banned the girls from entering the church while in ecstasy, Mary promptly complied, instructing the visionaries to adore the tabernacled Lord from outside instead.

She explained to them the meaning of the Mass, linking it closely with her Son's Good Friday immolation and encouraging devotion to the crucifix. Frequent Holy Communion was another constant theme. On those days when there was no Mass in the village church, Mary would arrange for the archangel Michael to give the seers Holy Communion in an invisible manner. In answer to the girls' request for a miracle to prove its authenticity, the Host given on a pre-announced occasion to Conchita (the principal seer) was visible; this prodigy was captured by a movie camera just a few feet away.

Another theme emphasized at Garabandal in conjunction with the Eucharist was the priesthood. In practically every apparition, the visionaries reported, they were urged to pray for priests. Mary was clearly all too aware of the crisis already spreading throughout the Church. The false "spirit of Vatican II" was starting to damage and diminish Eucharistic faith as well as allegiance to the Holy See, while the priest-drain was assuming worrying proportions worldwide.

A dramatic element of the Garabandal story is the promised miracle that will take place there in testimony to its dignified status as a Marian shrine. This miracle, Concita assures us (she alone knows the date and is to announce it eight days in advance), will be prodigious in itself and an occasion of healing for all the sick who are present. Moreover, it will serve to convert not only Russia but the whole world. Conchita further informs us that the miracle will take place on the feast of a Eucharistic martyr.

In view of Garabandal's intimate connections with the Blessed Sacrament, it is widely expected that the miracle's central motif will relate to the Eucharistic mysteries. Conceivably the miracle could even prove to be that very prodigy prophesied by Blessed Faustina: namely, the real-life Calvary scene of Christ's blood-stained crucifixion, which we mystically renew in the Mass, and now reproduced in giant proportions across the sky, shedding its illumination and merciful love upon our sinful world.

Medjugorje

Ever since the first of her daily apparitions in 1984 to six young people in this Bosnian village, the Queen of Peace, as Mary styles herself there, has strongly promoted devotion to her Son's sacramental sacrifice and his abiding presence in our tabernacles.

Right from the start, Gospa (the Croatian name for Our Lady) arranged for the public Mass to follow immediately on the Rosary and her apparition to the six visionaries. Thus the whole programme is happily integrated into the evening Eucharistic liturgy.

The Mass and its all-important role in our lives is emphasized again and again in Mary's Medjugorje messages. Here is a brief selection of her exhortations on the subject:

> The Mass is the greatest of all prayers.... You will never be able to grasp its grandeur and beauty.... You are to live the Mass.... The Mass is an experience of God.[11]

The final exhortation—"the Mass is an experience of God"—prompts the further reflection that the Medjugorje public Mass is no less an unforgettable *human* experience. For there is an overflow, multi-national congregation and often over 100 concelebrating priests. The atmosphere is one of intense faith and fervour, and the slow, melancholy Slav hymns linger long in the memory. Holy Communions reach record totals.

The chapel of perpetual adoration draws many pilgrims, including an encouraging number of young ones. The Queen of Peace frequently urges us to be generous in this devotion, reminding us, too, that she herself is ever co-adoring the fruit of her womb and winning rich graces for us.

Among those rich graces is her special Medjugorje gift of peace. This means primarily peace with the God of the commandments. It also means peace within ourselves, while its social expression stands for peace with others. Mary obtains this threefold peace for us from the Lamb of God we invoke in every Mass and receive in Holy Communion.

Another rich grace coming to us from the Medjugorje Virgin is an increase of faith, with a strong emphasis on Eucharistic faith. The mother of the Blessed Sacrament, who is blessed because of her believing, has helped many a pilgrim to believe more firmly and ardently in the mysteries of the altar. At the same time she exhorts pilgrims to deepen their knowledge and understanding of the faith—again with particular regard to the Eucharist.

Well-known and well-attested are the amazing signs in the sky that are of such frequent occurrence in Medjugorje. The shrine's Eucharistic dimension often manifests itself in what appears to be a sacred Host visible above the mountaintop cross or even above the spinning sun.

Betania

This takes us to what was a small farm not too distant from Caracas, the capital of Venezuela. Back in 1974, Maria Esperanza (the mystic and visionary central to the story) purchased this farm, which was destined to be the site of the apparitions that started in 1984 and have been drawing great pilgrim throngs ever since.

An unusual feature of these apparitions is that many pilgrims witness them, and do so without falling into a state of ecstasy. The local bishop—a Jesuit highly-trained in theology as well as being a professional psychologist—personally interviewed hundreds of these witnesses. After much research and reflection, he issued a pastoral endorsing the supernatural character of the apparitions.

In that same pastoral the bishop particularly welcomed the strong emphasis placed by Our Lady of Betania on Eucharistic life and frequent Confession. For, as he is aware, these sacramental treasures out-value by far the apparitions, the amazing signs in the sky (as at Medjugorje), and even the miraculous healings, wonderful and welcome though these phenomena are in themselves.

Another phenomenon connected with Betania is the so-called "miracle of the Eucharist." At a Midnight Mass celebrated on the feast of the Immaculate Conception in 1991, the 15,000-strong congregation saw a bright rose-coloured light above the newly-consecrated Host. On breaking it in half just before Communion, the celebrant was startled to see it was dripping blood.

That it was true human blood was subsequently confirmed by analysis in forensic laboratories. The bishop has testified that for three days the blood on the Host remained fluid before beginning to dry up. A further extraordinary circumstance is that the blood did not seep through the wafer-thin Host but left the other side exactly as it was before.

A fragment of that miraculous Host is now exposed in a monstrance in a convent chapel. With age the blood is now almost black in colour. But it remains a powerful stimulus for our Eucharistic faith—and comes to us as a gift from Our Lady of Betania.

The prodigy vividly brings home to us something of the bloodshed and torment of Calvary hidden beneath the sacramental veils but visible, even if only faintly, to the eyes of faith. Through these same eyes we also get a half-glimpse of Our Lady of Sorrows standing beside her Son as co-offerer and co-victim each time we break this bread and drink this cup (cf. 1 Cor. 10:16).

Many Other Marian Shrines

> One could perhaps speak of a specific geography of faith and Marian devotion, which includes all those special places of pilgrimage where the People of God seek to meet God's mother, in order to find within the radius of her maternal presence a strengthening of their own faith.[12]

In these words did Pope John Paul II refer to the numerous

Marian pilgrimage centres scattered across the world. Each has its own distinctive charism and character. And each is different in terms of background and importance. But in all of them Mary's underlying message to her pilgrim-children is one and the same: "Let me guide you to my Son, my Eucharistic Son."

Among the more illustrious Marian shrines one could and should mention in a general survey like this is the Miraculous Medal chapel in Paris, where Our Lady of the Blessed Sacrament gave her instructions to the young St. Catherine Labouré.

Then there are the two Belgian centres that remain a focus for many pilgrims: Beauraing and Banneux. More recently, the mother of God has favoured a small church in the Ukrainian village of Hrushiv as an apparition site. Also, the Korean town of Naju is currently associated with a weeping statue of Mary and some astounding Eucharistic miracles.

Finally there is the great and ancient Polish shrine of the so-called Black Madonna at Czestochowa, where Eucharistic devotion is particularly fervent. Fr. Michael O'Carroll has described this Marian sanctuary as "the hearth-stone of Polish Catholicism."[13] And, thanks to modern travel facilities, it is also becoming more and more a lodestone for pilgrims from other European countries and also overseas.

---

[1] Pope John Paul II: REDEMPTORIS MATER, 44

[2] Pope John Paul II: MARIAN MEDITATION AT A MASS IN CAPUA, 24 May 1992. (Reported in *L'Osserv. Romano*, 27 May 1992)

[3] Vatican II: LUMEN GENTIUM, 65

[4] Carlo Cardinal Martini: ADDRESS TO CLERGY IN 1994 (quoted in *Life Magazine*, December 1996, 50)

[5] St. Thomas Aquinas: cf. SUMMA CONTRA GENTILES, 4, 74, 7

[6] ST. JOHN DAMASCENE: PG 96, 953c

[7] John Henry Cardinal Newman: DISCOURSES TO MIXED CONGREGATIONS, 3rd Edit. (London) 1862, 429–430

[8] Jean Guitton: MOTHER OF THE REDEEMER, (London) 278

[9] Pope St. Pius X: AD DIEM ILLUM, 2 February 1904 AAS 36 (1903–4) 449–462

[10] Karl Rahner, S.J.: Quoted in "HAVE YOU FORGOTTEN FATIMA?" by Francis Johnston, CTS 1992

[11] WORDS FROM HEAVEN: Medjugorje Messages (Birmingham, Ala.) 5th Edit. (1985) 360

[12] Pope John Paul II: REDEMPTORIS MATER, 28

---

[13] Michael O'Carroll, C.S.Sp.: THEOTOKOS, Shrines of Our Lady, (Michael Glazier Inc.) 1982

CHAPTER TWELVE

Mary, Eucharist, Resurrection

In the preceding chapters we have been seeing from different angles how the Eucharist is the sacrament which, beyond all others, engages our Christian faith at the highest possible level. Indeed, it presents us with a feast of faith, even privileging us to meet and commune personally with Emmanuel himself—He who is faith's Giver as well as its final Goal.

We have also been seeing how the Eucharist, again beyond all others, is the sacrament of love. For the Saviour, whose sacrifice on our behalf represents the uttermost proof of his love, pours out under these sacred signs the treasures of his heart.

Now we are going to see in turn how the Eucharist, yet again to a supreme degree, is the sacrament of hope. For, in true hope-style, it points us towards things future and longed-for, making us at the same time confident that with God's help we shall attain and obtain them.

Now these things upon which Christian hope ultimately focuses can be summarized in one word: *resurrection*. That's certainly how St. Paul proceeded when defending himself before the Council in Jerusalem: "I stand on trial," he said, "because I am one who hopes for the resurrection of the dead" (Acts 23:6).

Basis of Our Belief

The basis of our own hoped-for resurrection is, of course, Our Lord's. To quote St. Paul again, the risen Jesus is himself "our hope" (1 Tim 1:1). And this our hope is literally embodied with his glorified humanity in the Eucharist, which is the living "memorial of his death and resurrection."[1] Moreover, He has promised bodily resurrection on the Last Day to those who partake sacramentally of his body and blood (cf. Jn. 6:39–40).

A further and powerfully supporting reason why we confidently hope in our own resurrection is that the Lord's mother has by his special favour already attained that status. Hence Mary acts as a prototype and model for our pilgrim selves still on the march along the roads of time. More than that, Mary floodlights the resurrection goal with her radiance as we plod our way onward and upward through this world's darkness. A liturgical prayer says encouragingly:

> Raised to the glory of heaven, the Blessed Virgin cares for the pilgrim Church with a mother's love, following its progress homeward until the day of the Lord dawns in splendour.[2]

The Risen Jesus

St. Teresa of Ávila states in her Autobiography that Our Lord, on those occasions she was privileged to behold him in the sacred Host, invariably revealed himself as the *risen* Saviour. Incidentally, He further revealed to her that on Easter morning He appeared in the first place to his mother, thereby confirming a Christian tradition going back to early centuries.

It is stimulating for our faith and devotion alike to recall that in the sacrament of the altar the God-Man's humanity is resurrected and glorified. That is to say, his body is no longer subject to suffering and death. Furthermore, it now reflects the divine splendour and beauty flowing from the Son of the Eternal Father.

Another endowment enjoyed by the risen Saviour's humanity is that it has been freed from the material limitations of life on earth; hence He can pass through closed doors and appear wheresoever He pleases. Finally, Our Lord's transformed body is completely under the sway of his human soul, of which it is now a fully apt and pliant co-principle of life and action. The technical name for this property of the Lord's body is *subtlety*.

Christ's Spiritual Body

St. Paul refers to Christ's risen body as being "spiritual" (1 Cor. 15:44). This does not imply that it is non-material, ethereal, incorporeal. Rather, "spiritual" signifies for St. Paul that a body is now within the sphere of divine power, light and holiness. At the same time he is affirming that the Saviour's body, albeit transfigured in heavenly glory, is verifiably identical with the one He had on earth.

Our Lord made this point very firmly in his first apparition to the assembled apostles. And, because it is such a key point, the gospel text deserves to be quoted in full:

> "Peace be upon you; it is myself; do not be afraid." They cowered down, full of terror, thinking that they were seeing an apparition. "Why," He said, "are you dismayed? Whence come these surmises in your hearts? Look at my hands and my feet, to be assured that it is myself. Touch me and see; a spirit has not flesh and bones, as you see that I have." And as He spoke thus, He showed them his hands and his feet. Then, while they were still doubting, and bewildered for joy, He asked them, "Have you anything here to eat?" So they put before him a piece of roast fish and a honeycomb; and He took these and ate in their presence, and shared his meal with them (Lk. 24:36–43).

Faith assures us that it is the selfsame risen Saviour who now sacramentally offers his life-sacrifice for us over and over again in the Mass, who offers himself to us in Communion as the bread of life, and who offers his perpetual presence for our adoration in the tabernacle. Faith assures us besides that "the Eucharist is the source and pledge of blessedness and glory for both soul and body."[3]

The Risen Mary

Now to see how Mary comes into the picture. She does so through her Assumption into heaven, that is, her bodily resurrection and definitive birth into the glory of paradise. The *Catholic Catechism* calls it "a singular participation in her Son's resurrection and an anticipation of the resurrection of other Christians."[4]

So Mary's body, which provided the source and womb of the God-Man's human life, now enjoys the same endowments as does his. Like him and with him she is now and forever in the world of resurrection radiance, unfading youth, and heavenly glory.

Thus the risen Mary represents for us wayfarers the dawn of salvation and glorious fulfilment. In her we see prefigured the destiny of the Church in general and, in particular, of each individual one of us. The mother of the Eucharist is now the pattern and paradigm of glorified mankind, the sign and icon of paradisal humanity.

Nor should we be at all surprised at Mary's privileged status. It was her initial Yes that allowed God to set in motion his mighty redemptive design: namely, a new covenant that would lead mankind to the brave new world of the resurrection and eternal glory. And it was Mary's hope-filled faith which made her confident that these and all God's promises would be fulfilled (cf. Lk. 1:45). Furthermore, the Blessed Virgin's co-redemptive role associated her most closely with her Son's lifework, especially on Calvary, where she stood alongside him as He suffered for our salvation and final resurrection.

Mary Promotes Our Hope

The risen Mary continues to stand alongside her Redeemer-Son in the sacrament of the altar. It is consoling to recall that she who bears the title "Mother of Fair Hope" keeps perpetual vigil before the Blessed Sacrament, ever ready to encourage her pilgrim children *en route* to the glorious world of the resurrection. In the *Salve Regina* we "poor banished children of Eve" hail the New Eve, mother of the Eucharist, as "our life, our sweetness and our hope." And we implore her to "show unto us, after this our exile, the blessed fruit" of her womb.

This our heavenly mother will certainly do, lovingly and graciously. But already here and now, that is, *during* our exile in this "vale of tears," she untiringly shows us the blessed fruit of her womb integrally present in the sacrament of the altar. As his handmaid and herald she urges us to draw ever closer to him. For not only is He the source of life and holiness; He is the pledge and pattern of our bodily resurrection when the new world finally dawns.

Our Own Resurrection

In the resurrection of Jesus, cause and exemplar of our own, we are meant to recognize the blueprint, the essential elements, of what our own humanity will be like after its transfiguration. Similarly, the Assumption of Mary is meant to throw light on the human condition after the resurrection. Her glorified state is an eschatological sign; that is, it bears on the "last things" in general, and on heaven in particular.

Christian faith and hope join voices in St. Paul's triumphant claim: "Christ will change our lowly body to be like his glorified body" (Phil. 3:21). Faith assures us that this is a prophetic statement of revealed truth. Hope reassures us that the risen Saviour will deliver on his great promise. Faith in the Eucharistic Emmanuel unites us with him on our journey. And hope in him gives us a cast-iron guarantee that our journey will be crowned with heavenly glory.

Our "Brother Body," as St. Francis of Assisi called it, will share in the heavenly glory due to envelop our entire selves. What a thrilling scenario this conjures up before the eyes of faith! Resurrected and glorified human beings will be forever freed from the bonds of sin, death and corruption. There will be no more pain or sickness; no more organisms wrecked and ruined by disease and deformity; no more pathetic lines of sick and suffering, crippled and disabled, such as await the Eucharistic Saviour's blessing in Lourdes. All Mary's children, no matter how broken their bodies, and despite the further ravages done to them by death and dissolution, will rise resplendent—as she already is—with the radiance of eternal life.

Christian hope's exciting vision of a risen humanity, far from being a mirage or wishful thinking, is a future reality anchored in our Eucharistic God and his mother ever alongside him. "Lord," runs the Church's prayer, "you give us new hope in the Eucharist."[5] He does indeed. Every Mass we attend, every Communion we receive, every minute we spend in adoration, implicitly expresses our confidence that He will one day share his risen life with us as He has already done with respect to his mother.

Mary and the Messianic Banquet

Being a devout daughter of Israel, Our Lady was closely familiar with its religious traditions and feasts. Prominent among these was the annual festival known as the Passover. It commemorated the Chosen People's deliverance from the bonds of slavery in Egypt and their safe passage across the Red Sea to the Promised Land.

The Passover ritual took the form of a family banquet at which a sacrificial lamb was eaten. The banquet was at the same time a memorial of past deliverance, a sign of God's present favour, and a pledge of future redemption through the promised Messiah. So the Passover was also in effect a Messianic banquet expressive of Israel's hopes and expectations.

The Messiah's mother was to play a leading role in the realization of those Old Testament hopes and expectations. The starting-point was her great act of faith at Nazareth. And a further great act of faith on her part was to be instrumental in setting up the Cana episode—the wedding-feast that was transformed into a Messianic banquet, which in turn foreshadowed the Messiah's Eucharistic banquet at the Last Supper.

That farewell banquet on Holy Thursday night followed faithfully the ritual prescribed for the Jewish Passover meal, thus fulfilling it and investing it with its definitive meaning.[6] The meaning in question is that the Eucharist is the true Messianic banquet, the Passover meal that celebrates our liberation from sin and death; it also supports our confident hope that we shall reach the Promised Land of risen life with the Saviour and his mother.

The Everlasting Messianic Banquet

Besides fulfilling the Jewish Passover, the Eucharist anticipates and prepares us for the final Passover of the Church into the glory of God's kingdom. That Passover will be the crowning and everlasting Messianic banquet, the culmination and goal of its predecessors. At the Last Supper Our Lord specifically referred to this glorious prospect in the world to come. The cup which He shared with his disciples, He said, was the symbol and pledge of the cup they would share with him at the heavenly banquet in his Father's kingdom (cf. Mt. 26:29; Lk. 22:16–18).

The Messiah's mother has already experienced her Passover to that world of the resurrection. Like her Son's, her glorification, in John Paul II's words, is "a premise and promise of our own glorification when we share in the risen Christ's feast of life."[7]

From her place near the risen Messiah's Eucharistic throne of grace the Virgin Mother points us to hope's bright horizons. For the Messianic banquet we attend at Mass is a prefiguration and pledge of the eternal banquet in our Father's kingdom.

Come, Lord Jesus!

A key word in the early Christian vocabulary was *Parousia*. In the original Greek it meant the visit of a royal person or high dignitary, and came to be applied to the glorious second coming of Christ. Scripture tells us that He will come in his glory to raise all mankind from the grave and judge them according to their works. He will also consummate the material universe (cf. Mt. 24:29–31; Rom. 8:22).

Maranatha was another key word among the first Christians. Addressed to the risen Saviour, it means: "Come, Lord Jesus!" And it conveys something of the expectancy, excitement and joy we Christians should feel towards the Parousia, that day of days in salvation history. St. Paul was enthusiastic about it:

> We are to look forward, blessed in our hope, to the day when there will be a new dawn of glory, the glory of the great God, the glory of our Saviour Jesus Christ (Tit. 2:13).

Eucharist and Parousia

Expectancy, excitement, joy over our coming resurrection are richly nourished in the mysteries of the Eucharist. Pope John Paul II is keenly aware of this:

> The Eucharist leads us to greater hope, for it is actually an ongoing proclamation of Christ's second glorious coming at the end of time ... and a hopeful encouragement for our advance to eternal life.[8]

On her long road from Pentecost to Parousia, the pilgrim Church never forgets for one moment that her Founder's sacramental presence and sacrifice are preparing her for the Passover into the Promised Land of eternal life. Thus in the Mass we declare that "we wait in joyful hope for the coming of Our Saviour Jesus Christ."[9] And we profess with St. Paul that "each time we break this bread and drink this cup we proclaim the death of the Lord *until He comes again*" (1 Cor. 11:26).

That same Lord has himself assured us that He will raise to eternal life those who receive his sacramental Body and Blood (cf. Jn. 6:54, 56). For this reason St. Ignatius of Antioch described Holy Communion as "the medicine of immortality."[10] The same idea was richly developed by Pope Leo XIII:

> The Eucharist is source and pledge of blessedness and glory, not for the soul alone, but for the body also.... In the frail and perishable body that divine Host, which is the immortal body of Christ, implants a principle of resurrection, a seed of immortality, which one day must germinate.[11]

Mary and the Parousia

That dynamic seed which is the Eucharist has already germinated in the mother of God, blossoming into a beauty beyond compare. Her sinless self now represents the first fruits of her Son's Parousia. As the New Eve, Mary is the dawn of glorious fulfilment for her human family, her multitudinous human family. And her maternal heart yearns to welcome every precious one of them into the new world of the City of God, the City of Mary.

Hence Our Lady's assiduous zeal in promoting Eucharistic devotion, particularly the regular reception of Holy Communion. For its special virtue is to nurture the seed of immortality within our mortal selves, preparing us for the glory to come. Christian hope it was that inspired Chesterton to write his memorable words:

> If seeds in the black earth can grow into such beautiful roses, what will not the heart of man become in his long journey to the stars?[12]

New Heaven and New Earth

It is intriguing to reflect that the Eucharistic Saviour we daily offer, receive and adore has clearly in mind the exact blueprint of the new world his divine power will inaugurate at his second coming. When that event transpires, we shall all share St. John's vision of the same:

> Then I saw a new heaven and a new earth. The old heaven and the old earth had vanished.... And I saw in my vision that holy city which is the new Jerusalem being sent down by God from heaven (Apoc. 21:1–2).

What this means is that, on the day of the Lord's coming there will take place, besides the resurrection of our bodies, a transfiguration of the material universe. St. Paul had a piercing intuition of this when he extended the dogma of the resurrection to the entire cosmos:

> If creation is full of expectancy, that is because it is waiting for the sons of God to be made known. The whole of nature, as we know, groans in a common travail all the while. Created nature has been condemned to frustration ... with a hope to look forward to: namely, that nature in its turn will be set free

> from the tyranny of corruption to share in the glorious freedom of God's sons.... And He who sat on the throne said, "Behold I make all things new" (Rom. 8:19–22; Apoc. 21:5).

It is entirely right and fitting that this good earth, the home that God has provided for our temporal life, should participate in our eternal glorification. Already it is represented in the elements of bread and wine we daily offer God along with ourselves. Moreover, this universe in its tranfigured state will be the dwelling-place, the habitat, the homeland, for the God-Man, his mother, and the great multitude of human and angelic blessed. St. John's mystical experience included an insight into this as well:

> I heard, too, a voice which cried aloud from the throne: Here is God's tabernacle pitched among men; He will dwell with them and they will be his own people, and He will be among them, their own God (Apoc. 21:3).

Queen of the Cosmos

Vatican II hailed Mary as "the image and beginning of the Church as it is to be perfected in the world to come."[13] And as Queen of the Cosmos (the title applied to Mary by St. Catherine Labouré) she is the image and beginning of all creation awaiting transformation at the Parousia. For, paradoxically, the mother of our Creator is herself one of his creatures—indeed, his masterpiece, the "paradigm of the art of God," as Balthasar said.

One of the most glowing tributes ever paid to the mother of all creation and model of its future sublimation came from an early Eastern theologian:

> God, wishing to create an image of absolute beauty, and to manifest clearly to angels and to men the power of his art, made Mary truly all-beautiful.... He made of her a blend of all divine, angelic and human perfections, a sublime beauty embellishing the two worlds, rising from earth to heaven and surpassing

even the latter.[14]

The queen of heaven and earth stands as the pattern and icon of risen humanity and the paradisal world, because she is at the heart of the Incarnation and subsequently the Eucharistic life of her Son. Equally she is at the heart of God's creation and its coming transfiguration. Few have expressed this truth as eloquently as did Cardinal Suenens:

> God, the incomparable artist, willed the whole creation in view of Christ and consequently in view of Mary, since in the divine plan Christ was not conceived without Mary. For her sake was created the brilliance of the sun, the fairyland of the stars and planets, as ornaments of her glory. For her, the earth was a footstool; for her were made the mountains and plains, the oceans and rivers; and the blue sky was to be the image of her queenly mantle. All was for her, because she is the first-born of creatures in Christ.[15]

The Heavenly Assembly

So in the Eucharist—this great sacrament of hope—we actually have with us, in person, the Creator of the new world ahead, with its future queen and mother ever at his side. The alliance of their hearts is focused with longing on that glorious day when we, their beloved redeemed, will achieve our true destiny as citizens of the heavenly City.

Representative of every nation on earth and from every age of history, its citizens will be mustered for the first time when the Lord comes in his glory. John Donne thus describes that dramatic moment:

> At the round earth's imagin'd corners, blow
> Your trumpets, angels, and arise, arise
> From death, you numberless infinities
> Of souls, and to your scatter'd bodies go.[16]

In the new world of the resurrection, death, suffering, sorrow and want will have passed away forever. So, too, will the weakness and trials of old age. For the risen life transcends the conditions of time as well as space; consequently we shall be blessed, perpetually and unlosably, with the vigour and beauty of youth.

Banquet of Life

As for our human spirits, they will rejoice in the beatific vision. Pius XII said apropos of this:

> In that beatific vision it will be granted to the eyes of the human mind, strengthened by the light of glory, to contemplate the Father, the Son and the Holy Spirit in an utterly ineffable manner.[17]

This is the heavenly banquet of which Scripture speaks so often, and which is foreshadowed so strikingly in the Eucharist. It is the banquet of beatitude; our minds and hearts will feast forever on the fullness of God's perfections—his truth, his wisdom, his goodness, his omnipotence, his beauty, his love.

This heavenly feast is the bread of angels—in other words, the enjoyment of the beatific vision and intimate communion with the three Divine Persons. The mother of the Eucharist is already enjoying that experience as are the blessed spirits, both angelic and human.

St. Teresa of Ávila affirms unat Eucharistic faith and hope will unerringly lead us "to rejoice one day with our Beloved in a happiness and rapture that can never end."[18] And Cardinal Newman, for whom the promise of the resurrection was a lifelong inspiration, frequently dwelt on that prospect. Here is a prayer he composed about it:

> Each of us, soul and body, shall be plunged into the abyss of glory which surrounds the Almighty ... we shall see him, and share his blessedness.... It is the occupation of eternity, ever new, inexhaustible, ineffably ecstatic, the stay and blessedness of existence,

> thus to drink in and be dissolved in Thee.[19]

Anticipations of Heaven

Having been raised at Baptism to new supernatural life, we must, St. Paul exhorts us, "seek the things that are above, where Christ is seated at the right hand of God" (Col. 3:1). He also reminds us that "our conversation is in heaven" (Phil. 3:20).

For this reason St. Augustine described Christians as "Easter people." Though still in our world of time, we already reach out beyond life's horizon to God's eternal kingdom. We anticipate here below the everlasting good things to come.

We do this in a very powerful way by means of the Eucharistic mysteries. Through the Mass, the *Catechism* teaches, "we already unite ourselves with the heavenly liturgy and anticipate eternal life."[20] The Holy Father constantly returns to this theme. Addressing a youth rally in Seville, he said:

> Our life is rooted in this mystery of faith. And it leads to greater hope, because the Eucharist is an ongoing proclamation of his glorious second coming ... a hope-filled encouragement for our advance to eternal life.[21]

Leading the heavenly liturgy is its queen—the mother of the Eucharistic Christ. It is the liturgy of adoration, worship and praise. And Mary, the prime adorer, worshipper and giver of praise, actually leads that sublime liturgy ***here before our tabernacles***. Therefore every minute we spend with the Eucharistic Jesus unites us directly with Mary and the entire court of heaven.

We saw earlier how Holy Communion anticipates very vividly and realistically the realities of the eternal world, also pledging our future possession of its treasures. For through Christ's sacred body and blood "the seed of immortal life is planted in the frailty of our human flesh."[22]

Miraculous Anticipation of Heaven

There have been a number of well-authenticated cases in Church history of certain mystics actually being privileged to subsist for years on end *solely on the Eucharist*. That is to say, they live without taking anything solid or liquid because they derive their bodily sustenance exclusively—and miraculously—from Holy Communion.

Hereby these chosen souls bear striking witness to the truth and power of the Blessed Sacrament. At the same time, their bodies, though still pre-resurrection and therefore mortal, nevertheless anticipate, by their absolute abstinence from food or drink of any kind, something of the condition our risen humanity will enjoy when the Eucharistic Jesus comes as the Lord of the Parousia.

To that extent, therefore, these "total abstainers" signpost for us the coming resurrection. For it will usher in a glorified world where the all-satisfying nourishment for our body-soul selves will be the Bread of Angels; that is, our unbroken and intimate communion with the Eternal Word in the bosom of the Trinity—the very communion, indeed, which the glorified humanity of the Word's mother is enjoying now and forever

A prominent name among those who lived for a number of years on the Eucharist alone is St. Catherine of Siena, who died in 1380. Another canonized example was St. Nicholas of Flue, patron saint of Switzerland; his absolute fast is said to have lasted for 20 years until his death in 1487. Venerable Anne Catherine Emmerich, the German mystic, subsisted on the Eucharist alone for 12 years before she died in 1824.

In modern times there have been several well-documented instances of this Eucharistic prodigy. For such it is. He who is the Resurrection and the Life nourishes not only their souls but their bodies through his sacramental Self. Italian-born Luisa Piccarreta subsisted in this manner for as many as 65 years, and the French mystic, Martha Robin, for 30.

Two Prominent Examples

The first is the German stigmatist Teresa Neumann; for some 40 years preceding her death in 1962 she subsisted entirely on daily Communion, only ingesting a small quantity of water when unable to swallow the Host. Yet, despite her total fast and the further fact that she regularly shed copious amounts of blood in her stigmatic experiences, she astonishingly never lost any weight; on the contrary, she steadily put it on, registering 218 pounds on the scales in 1953 as opposed to the 121 pounds she weighed in 1927. Nor was there any question of fraud or deceit about all this; careful surveillance and observation ruled out such explanations.

Another prominent example is the Portuguese stigmatist, Alexandrina da Costa. For her last 12 years on earth (she died in 1955) she lived exclusively on the bread of life. Noteworthy about her case is the rigorous and vigilant observation to which she was subjected by relays of nurses and doctors in an Oporto hospital. Alexandrina was kept in isolation for a whole month. But during that time their strict surveillance failed to detect the least sign of fraudulence. It was proved beyond doubt that Holy Communion, and it alone, was her daily food. Moreover, Alexandrina's physical and mental condition remained as balanced as before. The medical authorities conceded that the phenomenon had no possible natural explanation.

Alexandrina had in common with all other known cases of her kind a deep and tender devotion to the mother of the Eucharist. St. Augustine's words about God's mother would surely hold an extra significance for these chosen souls: "She gave milk to our Bread."[23]

Homesick for Heaven

St. Ignatius relates in his spiritual diary that during Mass he was frequently given, along with visions of the Trinity and Our Lady, vistas of heaven, our true home and fatherland. And this experience, he says, made him long and yearn for that blessed fulfilment of our Christian hopes and desires.

The liturgy is impregnated with this same idea. "Father," the

Church prays, "may our Holy Communions help us to love heaven. May its promise and hope guide our way on earth." And the Opening Prayer in the Mass of the Assumption makes these petitions:

> Father, may we see heaven as our final goal and come to share Mary's glory.... May we who receive the sacrament of salvation be led to the glory of heaven by the prayers of the Virgin Mary.[24]

So the Eucharist is the great sacrament of hope, and the Mother of the Eucharist is a God-given icon and beacon for us wayfarers and pilgrims heading for home. For Mary is the living link between our sinful selves and the God-Man "who has turned all our sunsets into dawns."

Finally, let us ask the mother of the Blessed Sacrament to obtain for us what was so liberally bestowed upon little Jacinta of Fatima: the grace to long and yearn to be with Jesus and herself in our heavenly home, our true native land; and the further grace to be generous with God, especially in making sacrifices, so that many precious souls may be helped to reach that same glorious destiny.

Gerard Manley Hopkins has given exquisite expression both to our longing for heaven and the confidence we have in the Mystical Rose, our Mother of Fair Hope and Mother of the Eucharistic Jesus:

> In the gardens of God, in the daylight divine,
> Find me a place by thee, mother of mine.
> In the gardens of God, in the daylight divine,
> I shall come home to thee, mother of mine.
> In the gardens of God, in the daylight divine,
> Show me thy Son, mother, mother of mine.
> In the gardens of God, in the daylight divine,
> I shall worship his wounds with thee, mother of mine.[25]

---

[1] Vatican II: PRESBYTERORUM ORDINIS, 5

---

[2] Preface: VOTIVE MASS OF THE BLESSED VIRGIN MARY, IMAGE AND MOTHER OF THE CHURCH
[3] Pope Leo XIII: MIRAE CARITATIS, AAS 34 (1902)
[4] CATECHISM OF THE CATHOLIC CHURCH: (Veritas) 1994 #966
[5] ROMAN MISSAL: 31st Sunday of the Year: Post-Communion Prayer
[6] cf. CATECHISM OF THE CATHOLIC CHURCH: (Veritas) 1994 #1340
[7] Pope John Paul II: ADDRESS ON 6 APRIL 1997 (Reported *in L'Osserv. Romano*, 9 April 1997)
[8] Pope John Paul II: ADDRESS ON 31 OCTOBER 1983 (Reported in *L'Osserv. Romano*, 6 November 1983)
[9] ROMAN MISSAL: Rite of Communion
[10] St. Ignatius of Antioch: LETTER TO THE EPHESIANS, 20, 2
[11] Pope Leo XIII: op. cit.
[12] G. K. Chesterton: THE RETURN OF DON QUIXOTE, (New York) 1927, 170
[13] Vatican II: LUMEN GENTIUM, 68
[14] Gregory Palamas: quoted in THEOTOKOS, by Michael O'Carroll, C.S.Sp., (Michael Glazier) 1982, 162–163
[15] Léon-Joseph Cardinal Suenens: MARY, THE MOTHER OF GOD (London) 1956, 21
[16] John Donne: HOLY SONNETS, 7
[17] Pope Pius XII: MYSTICI CORPORIS, 80
[18] St. Teresa of Ávila: EXCL. 15, 3
[19] John Henry Cardinal Newman: MEDITATIONS AND DEVOTIONS, Introd. by Meriol Trevor, (London) 1964, 128, 95
[20] CATECHISM OF THE CATHOLIC CHURCH: (Veritas) 1994 #1326
[21] Pope John Paul II: ADDRESS AT EUCHARISTIC CONGRESS, Seville, 1983 (Reported in *L'Osserv. Romano*, 23 June 1983)
[22] Pope John Paul II: ADDRESS ON 2 JUNE 1983 (Reported in *L'Osserv. Romano*, 5 June 1983)
[23] St. Augustine: SERMON 184, 2, 3 PL 38, 997
[24] FIRST SUNDAY OF ADVENT: POST-COMMUNION PRAYER
[25] Gerard Manley Hopkins: ROSA MYSTICA: Poems and Prose, selected by W. H. Gardner (Penguin) 1966

About the Author

Fr. Richard Foley, S.J.

Fr. Richard Foley, S.J., belongs to the British Province of the Society of Jesus and is based at the well-known Farm Street church in London. After obtaining his theology doctorate in Louvain, he taught the subject in a seminary for a number of years.

Fr. Foley has written many articles for religious publications and is the author of *The Drama of Medjugorje*. He is famous for his eloquent and enthusiastic talks at conferences, retreats, and parish missions on both sides of the Atlantic. In addition to experience in print media and in-person, Fr. Foley has been well received by broadcast media audiences, including several series for EWTN.